GW00985775

Jenny Selby-Green began her ca
1950s when she joined her local newspaper as a junior reporter.
She worked on several provincial weeklies and magazines as a
reporter, columnist and editor. She now lives in Chipping Norton
where her involvement with West Oxfordshire Writers, the theatre
writing group and the Chipping Norton Literary Festival
influenced her decision, after she was widowed,
to come out of retirement and start again.

TO BED ON THURSDAYS

Jenny Selby-Green

MOSAÏQUEPRESS

First published in the UK in 2013 by
MOSAÏQUE PRESS
Registered office:
70 Priory Road
Kenilworth, Warwickshire CV8 1LQ
www.mosaïquepress.co.uk

Printed in the UK.

ISBN 978-1-906852-17-7

CONTENTS

INTRO

WRITING THESE reminiscences has brought back an unbelievable number of memories; most, fortunately, are pleasant in that 'did we really do that?' kind of way. The answer is 'yes... mostly.' With the passage of time, memory becomes an unreliable witness, so some of these may not be a hundred per cent accurate. In certain cases, that's definitely a blessing in disguise.

Although most of what I am about to describe took place in and around Aylesbury in Buckinghamshire, where I got my first job in newspapers, I worked over the years on five other local papers in that county, in Suffolk and in Oxfordshire. For convenience and simplicity, I have taken liberties with the geography of that delightful part of England, removed some incidents from their original setting and transposed others in time and place to suit my narrative.

So anyone with long and crystal-clear recall can safely deny that any event that I describe ever happened on their paper, or if they wish it had, they may claim it with confidence. I am not about to question someone else's memory when my own has its blind spots.

Those days just seem incredibly ancient history, especially in today's context of fast, disposable news. It was of course more than sixty years ago, and the revolution in news gathering, writing and distribution, not to mention what actually is news, has changed forever how things are done.

Where local papers remain, they're printed by completely different methods. The flatbed press has disappeared except in museums, and with it probably some of the characters, the stories and the camaraderie as well. Are we the poorer for it? You be the judge. Let me invite you to take your smart phone earpiece out, forget the internet and social media for awhile and turn the pages on another era.

JSG

Chipping Norton, 2013

– 1 –

YOUNG MAN, SOME TYPING

IT WAS A very small classified advertisement buried deep in the weekly *Herald*. I don't know why it caught my eye because it looked more like a filler at the bottom of the Sits Vac column than an offer of gainful employment. It read:

> Position as trainee reporter offered to young man, finished
> National Service, with shorthand and some typing skill.
> Enthusiasm and fitness essential.

I read it several times and tried on the qualifications for fit. Enthusiasm, well that was me to a T, and what seventeen-year-old wasn't fit? This was the 1950s: war rationing had just ended, labour-saving devices had yet to invade most homes, sports were still a sacrosanct part of school curriculum and leisure mostly meant some form of strenuous outdoor activity like gardening or hill walking. No, fitness was not an issue. And I'd already learned shorthand and touch typing, and had the certificates to prove it.

The more I thought about 'trainee reporter', the more the idea grew on me. I read a lot and quite enjoyed writing. There was only one small problem that I could see, and that was the word 'man'. I mulled this over awhile. Clearly they didn't have me in mind. Well, I thought, nothing ventured.

I wrote out a letter of application in the terribly-terribly proper style of the time (my but we could write letters) and then laboriously made a neat copy of the original which was in my normal illegible scrawl, posted it off and waited hopefully. Shortly an interview summons came back with a date and time. Either the Editor was impressed by my keenness, ability to type and take shorthand, or there had been a singular lack of young men applying. It mattered little. I started preparing myself mentally, not by rehearsing answers to the questions I might be asked in the interview but, as with most girls of that bygone era, puzzling over what I should wear.

THE *HERALD* occupied a Victorian building near the railway station. Years of soot and smoke from steam engines had turned the bricks black, and the small windows were smeared and dirty. I crept into the reception hall, holding the Editor's letter before me like a flashlight. The hall was decidedly dingy and smelt strongly of what I was to realise later was the heady whiff of printers' ink. On my left was a small hatch. I knocked on it. The glass panel shot up with a screech and a man's head peered through. I thrust the letter towards him.

"This is Classifieds," he said abruptly, "you want Editorial." He waved towards another door opposite and brought the panel down with a whack.

I gave the door a feeble, tentative knock and waited. Nothing. I tried again, a little louder. "Enter," commanded a voice from within. I did as told. Behind an imposing oak desk sat the owner of the voice, Mr Harry Godber, a small sandy-haired man in a dark suit who by his bearing and stern look was definitely The Editor with a capital E (and when in full flow, a capital T too). Ranged floor to ceiling around him were shelves containing bound copies of the *Herald* which even in the early 1950s had been established for more than a hundred years. His desk, however, was disappointingly clear except for a telephone, a blotter and an inkpot. Where was the typewriter and green eyeshade which all Hollywood films of newspaper offices had prepared me for?

A single wooden chair sat in front of the desk. I positioned myself gingerly on it and the interview began. I say interview; it felt more like an inquisition under the Editor's glare. Somehow I stumbled through a list of questions. Mr Godber explained that journalism was one of the very few professions where men and women had equal pay, "so that means you have to work really hard and give one hundred per cent to us." In exchange for my loyalty and service, he was prepared to pay me the juniors' rate of £3 a week, from which of course came deductions for National Insurance and income tax. But there was something called the

Cost of Living Allowance. This was a flat rate that all staff, including the Editor, received. "You'll be getting well over a pound a week," he said. I did a quick mental calculation and realised that my pay would be considerably less than the County Council had given me to do nothing in my previous employment. He made passing reference to extras such as expenses and lineage, which would also enhance my pay. I didn't like to ask what lineage was because he was still talking.

"I didn't advertise for a girl because they all go off and get married, and the *Herald* does not employ married women," Mr Godber said, without the slightest embarrassment. He told me he would expect me to stay at least two years. "It takes that time for you to be any use to us," he explained. "That is why we don't want ambitious young men who have their hearts set on Fleet Street. Nor are we going to have you going off to the *Courier*" – he spat out the name of our weekly rival as it clearly left a bad taste in the mouth – "once you've learnt the ropes here, and they offer you a bit more money or a column of your own, after we've trained you."

The Editor proceeded to explain the work rapidly and quite incomprehensibly, using a great many terms whose meaning I could only guess at. He barked out his words with the rapidity of a Maxim gun firing round after round.

Interview over, he marched me back into the dingy hallway, where my brightly patterned cotton dress with its full skirts bulked out by net petticoats was as out of place as an exotic bird and in marked (and not entirely approving) contrast to the white shirts and bland ties adopted by Mr Godber and the Advertisement Manager, Mr Cardew Carruthers. Mr Godber indicated a door at the far end of the hall. "That leads to the printing works," he said, without further explanation. He led the way around a corner to a narrow and rickety wooden staircase with bare wooden treads. The landing of the dogleg was very small, and almost blocked with tottering stacks of newspapers. In later days, I realised this was the only exit from upstairs and a considerable fire risk. The *Courier* would have had a wonderful scoop when we were all burnt to a frazzle on the first floor, but since Health and Safety regulations had yet to be invented, there was no story until such a calamity actually happened. As it was, the upstairs was empty of people; the paper was published on Thursday evening and Friday was the half-day.

We peered briefly into a small room where the mysteriously named reader and his boy worked at a table with two wooden chairs. A well-thumbed OED, a couple of almanacs, several district directories and an atlas dating from before the war occupied one shelf on a large wooden bookcase; dozens of envelopes were arranged on the others. This I later learned was the library and filing system. The next door opened onto to a larger room, which Mr Godber told me grandly was the reporters' room. At the end of the passage was a third room, for the sub-editor and the chief reporter. The final closed door I correctly assumed led to the sole lavatory.

"Start on Monday," Mr Godber said as we renegotiated the steep staircase. And that was that. It was a moment or two before I realised I had got the job. But the Editor was still talking. "No trousers allowed," he said, then suddenly he turned gloomy. "I don't suppose you'll last long. None of the girls do. It's the evening and Saturday jobs and the long hours. It was different in my day. My father paid a premium to the proprietor, so I had to stick to the job until he got his money's worth."

I beat a rather hasty retreat so he didn't have time to consider imposing a similar condition on my own parents.

THAT'S HOW my career in journalism began. Career! No one had ever suggested that a career might await me. What a novel idea. Of course, like every young English woman in the early 1950s, I was expected to work at a job – until I married. At Queen Anne's at Caversham, my all-girls boarding school, the deputy head sat us down one spring day of our final year and suggested that a very few brainy girls might aim for a university place, while others should think about training to be nurses or teachers. And that was about it for careers advice. She spent much of our half-hour session romanticising about the advantages of being a teacher – and got little thanks for it.

As an afterthought, she suggested the rest of us should learn shorthand and typing. "You can become secretaries – if you're good enough." Thank you, Miss, for such a boost to our confidence.

So I had left school at sixteen with a half-dozen of the new O-levels to show for an expensive education, and a place at the St George's Secretarial College for Young Ladies in Great Portland Street in London. It offered a gruelling course in Pitman shorthand, touch typing, elementary book-keeping and of course spelling, punctuation and grammar, as well as good manners and politeness. We banged typewriters in time to music to help us learn to type at a speed of at least forty words a minute. As for shorthand, we were expected to be able to take dictation at a hundred and twenty words a minute.

A few months into this particular purgatory, my father – who was Bucks County Welfare officer responsible for what was then called Public Assistance – told me he'd heard there was a vacancy for a junior clerk in the Education Department. "Get yourself onto the council's books and you'll never be out of a job," was his philosophy. So I left the college one Thursday lunchtime, went for an interview on the Friday, and started work on the Monday.

Did I say college was purgatory? That was nothing compared to my new job. Boring doesn't come close to describing it. I didn't need the painfully learned shorthand as my boss dictated a letter so slowly that it was easier to write it in longhand, and even then with time for the odd doodle and embellishment. We seemed to spend most of the morning waiting for the rattle of the tea trolley coming down the corridor. When it reached our door, I was despatched to get his morning coffee and biscuit, and then to return the dirty cup and saucer. The best thing about the 11am tea trolley was that its departure meant it would soon be time for lunch, but then in mid-afternoon it made a repeat appearance, this time for tea and cakes. I could almost feel my brain cells turning into tapioca.

After three months of this, I was ready for anything when my friend Jean suggested that we go on one of the new package tours and fly to Majorca for a week's holiday. I had never flown or been abroad: this would be quite an adventure. Father and Mother were apprehensive but after speaking to Jean's parents, the adults decided they would allow us to go. We went off to apply for passports in a state of high excitement.

Then I asked my boss if I could have a week's holiday in three months time. The answer was an emphatic 'No'. Holiday allowances were not given until after a year's employment.

There was no way out. I was sacked just before the holiday. Apparently my job was so important that they couldn't spare me for a week without pay. I wondered who they would train to take over the coffee and tea duties and type the odd letter. I later learned two girls had been employed and set to work on the filing.

Our Mediterranean holiday was wonderful. I came back bronzed and ready to bend everyone's ear about the delights of sun, sangria and somewhere other than England, but also broke and jobless. My immediate prospects didn't look bright. The market in the mid-Chilterns for shorthand typists with very little experience and a poor reference was limited, not to say non-existent. But the good old Labour Exchange still managed to find a couple of openings.

The first job they sent me for was with the local Pig Marketing Board. Even at the interview, the odour accompanying the farmers coming and going through the dreary reception hall where I and the other candidates sat and waited was enough to turn my stomach. "You'll get used to it in no time," said the man doing the interviews. No I won't, I thought. Besides, I had absolutely no interest or knowledge of pigs except as two crispy rashers laid neatly beside a fried egg. Somehow I must have appeared more enthusiastic than I felt because they offered me the position of junior clerk. Naturally I turned it down.

Then I had an interview in a factory. A fierce woman explained about the job but it was so noisy I could hardly hear what she said, nor could I understand what they made, and the test document she gave me to type made no sense at all. But again the letter arrived confirming the job; again I replied in the negative, aware that I was leaving myself little room for manoeuvre.

That was because Direction of Labour was still in force, left over from wartime regulations. I knew that the next interview the Labour Exchange set up for me would be crucial. If I were offered that job, I would have to take it because I had already been accepted for two positions and turned them down. The law stipulated that I would get no benefits of any kind if I didn't take the third job, whatever it might turn out to be.

Hence my reading of the situations vacant column in the local paper and why almost out of desperation I had applied to become a reporter. The idea of the freedom from being in an office all day was a definite attraction.

MY FIRST DAY was decidedly dull. I arrived on the dot of nine as instructed, wearing a dark skirt and white blouse, and was surprised to find myself again the only one on the upstairs floor. But there were rumblings and men's voices from the basement. I hung my coat on the hook at the back of the door, where it joined a black trilby and a black beret draped round with a black tie (which I later found out was the communal funeral outfit), and sat nervously at the side of a large table in the reporters' room.

The room had a lived-in feel about it. One wall was painted beige and had telephone numbers scribbled over it. On the facing wall was a large map of the district with a smaller street plan of Aylesbury, assorted pin-ups and calendars tacked to it. The sole window was clearly not for opening, although its top fanlight yielded a small distance. Pushed against the window was a large dining table with a leather-cloth top deeply torn, scratched and inky. Reposing in the middle of the table was a black telephone, pads of blank white paper, a box with a few sheets of carbon paper and two large and ancient typewriters. Three wooden chairs, one of them all but hidden under a tottering pile of the other local newspapers, were pulled up to the table.

In the unoccupied corner was a small and tidy desk. This was

The old Herald offices, demolished to make way for a multi-storey carpark in 1966.

the first one occupied as John Smythe, the sports editor, strode in with a cheery "How do?" He looked the part. In his youth he had been a sprinter, and he still insisted that he kept warm by running everywhere. Even in the depths of winter, he would arrive clad in sports jacket without scarf or gloves.

Despite his many accomplishments, he had never mastered a typewriter and was the only reporter allowed to file his reports in longhand. Nearly all day John would hunch over his private desk turning out reams of copy in his immaculate copperplate style, using a dip pen and an inkwell. The compositors always insisted they couldn't read any one else's writing. When he retired, someone worked out that he had written so much copy it would stretch to London and back.

John lived about six miles away in Tring where, as with many of the small towns nearby, the *Herald* had a sub-office. To save money, John acted as courier. He was also a keen gardener and was apt to appear carrying a sack containing a few items of news plus apples or plums for his co-workers. His home produce went into the thick salad and onion sandwiches his wife made him in the summer and the home-made vegetable soup that filled his Thermos flask in winter. All of this he consumed at his desk, because he didn't take a lunch hour like the rest of us. His last bus home went at 5pm so at 4.45pm he scuttled out and began his run to the bus depot while the rest of us laboured on for at least another half-hour.

AYLESBURY HAD a factory called the Bif, short for the Bifurcated & Tubular Rivet Company, whose importance in our county town went far beyond metal fasteners. The Bif marked time for us with its works siren. When the seven o'clock went off, it woke us clerical workers as well as the factory workers who would have to get in for eight o'clock. The noon one signalled their dinner hour while we had to wait for the one o'clock to get our luncheon. The last siren would shriek across the town at 5pm which I quickly learned meant there was only another half hour to rush through piles of work. How different from working in local government where the last hooter meant clearing of desks and doing nothing until it was time to leave.

Some time after nine the other two reporters, Len and Stan,

came in. "This is Jen," said John by way of introduction as we began the daily panto around the seating arrangements. Throughout my time on the paper, we played a type of Mad Hatters' tea party with the two typewriters, two useable chairs and three people. Two of the chairs were all right though not comfortable, but the third was wobbly. We preferred to use it as a repository for the old papers but had to press it into service when we were all in the room together. Extraordinary though it seems now, nobody during my time there thought to ask management if we could have another chair or even cushions.

I was absorbing the chair situation when a third man appeared. This was Dave, the junior reporter I was to replace. He was working out his week's notice.

He ignored me. "God's just coming in," he announced dramatically. 'God', it transpired, was what they called our Editor, Mr Godber, because "his word is law." Immediately Len and Stan rolled paper into the old Underwood typewriters and began pounding away. The noise was deafening. Then one held up his hand. Now I could hear the telephone ringing. Obviously no one could hear a word if anyone was typing. But John was able to carry on writing in longhand, and the scratch of the nib suddenly sounded loud.

Dave picked up the receiver. "Reporters," he said with impressive authority. The voice at the other end was giving out something. "No, sorry," he interrupted, "I can't take orders for printing. You've got the wrong office." He reeled off another telephone number and finished by saying, "No, I can't put you through sorry," and hung up.

Seeing my look of bafflement, Dave explained that the newspaper had one number and four extensions, so the phone would ring simultaneously in four rooms – ours, the sub-editor's, Mr Godber's and the Classified office.

"God never answers the phone," he added. "So if it's for him you have to jiggle the bar until someone else answers and apologise to the person on the other end. If Classified answer, Bert will go across the hall to tell God. But every so often it's someone who is trying to get wedding invitations printed, or wants to know if their posters are ready. That's the other office in the Market Square. We can ring them on their number but we can't put calls through. People don't understand and can get quite shirty with us."

I made a silent vow that unless I was alone in the room (which seemed unlikely as John was always there) I wouldn't answer the phone until I understood a bit more.

"John never answers the telephone except at lunchtime, and then you'll find half a message for you with no number to ring back usually," Dave added, obviously trying to be helpful. The scratching pen sounded louder still.

Footsteps sounded on the wooden staircase, and once again the typewriters took a bashing. Mr Godber put his head round the door. "Okay then, Miss?" he said. "Ask Pete or Bill if you need anything." He disappeared and went into the next room.

"He won't call you by name for ages," Len told me. "He always reckons new female staff will be out in weeks."

WITHIN A FEW days, I realised that this was the regular start to the day from Monday to Thursday. The Editor came in to a cacophony of sound and frantic business, usually with the phone ringing. Having removed his cycle clips, and propped up his bicycle in the entrance hall, he would go into his office in case there was anything waiting for his attention on the desk. Then he would come upstairs and into the next room, look at the big diary (referred to as the bible), note the events of the day and who Pete, the chief reporter, had pencilled in to cover them. Then he and the sub-editor, Bill, would both go downstairs for what they called the daily press conference which terminated regularly when the tea tray arrived about ten minutes later.

Bill was a dour man with a careworn, worried expression. He gave out an impression of a great deal of greyness from the ground up. His trousers were a mid-grey flannel, his sweater a lighter tone hand-knit with the shoulders dusted with dandruff from his thin grey hair. A more liberal helping of grey sprinkled the front of the sweater where ash fell from the cigarette stuck permanently (or so it seemed) to his lower lip.

The room he shared with Pete was always wreathed in cigarette smoke from both men. Bill habitually sat with a large overflowing ashtray of butts close by his left hand while his right held the dreaded blue pencil as he read through, slashed out and corrected parts of the reporters' copy. Usually there was either a half-smoked or fresh cigarette tucked behind one ear and a spare pencil stub behind the other.

One Thursday evening, when everyone was working frantically to get the paper to bed, and just as the last copy was being subbed, there was a scream from Bill. Somehow he had put a lit fag behind his ear, and managed to set his hair alight. That was one dramatic story that didn't make the pages of our rather dull weekly newspaper although it certainly added a spark to our evening.

It needn't have been dull, I often reflected. We had ample opportunity, judging by the variety of invitations that came in, to make it interesting. Pete entered all the functions in our bible, as well as the regular events such as Magistrates' Court hearings, council meetings and the vast number of Saturday events. Throughout the year, these varied from the summer flower and agricultural shows to the winter Christmas fairs, jumble sales and carol concerts.

The real reason it was dull was because that was how our proprietor wanted it. He had inherited the newspaper and the printing works from his great-grandfather who had founded it and been its first editor and sole staff for many years. Our proprietor knew nothing about printing or newspapers, but liked to have the first paper off the press on a Thursday evening. Occasionally he would wander round the printing works or be closeted with the Editor but he never made it to the first floor.

Most of the time he was worried that the *Herald* might lose money, and felt it would be better to concentrate on the lucrative printing business, whose staff supported that idea – as well they might. He was always frightened that he might have to subsidise the paper from his other business: he co-owned the biggest haberdashers in Aylesbury. Naturally all his advertisements were free, so it was actually the other way around: the paper in its own small way subsidised the other business.

There was also his permanent fear that the paper might be involved in a lawsuit, or might offend one of his friends from the Chamber of Commerce. So the *Herald* had a mild and middle-of-the-road attitude to everything, despite God occasionally trying to slip in a controversial leader and stir up the circulation and the number of Letters to the Editor.

The proprietor had a few other odd ideas. One was that he could achieve economies by curtailing tea drinking on the premises. He employed an ancient retainer named Joss as general dogsbody. Joss was responsible for driving the van, packing up the papers for delivery and cleaning the works. He also made the tea on the understanding that it was strictly one cup for everyone morning and afternoon. Anyone missing at 10am and 3pm would go without. This was hardest for the reporters who often had to leave the office for an assignment just before the tea break. Nor were we allowed to take in our own instant coffee and brew up for ourselves. The proprietor considered that this would lead to the staff drinking coffee all day, and therefore doing no work.

Joss was whole-heartedly on the side of the proprietor, although for an entirely different reason. He didn't see why making tea had to be his job. Nevertheless, he did it with a miserly precision that would have impressed Ebenezer Scrooge himself. He could measure the water in the kettle with such accuracy that he was certain there would be just sufficient for one mug of tea per person. He even toured the reporters' room twice a day to ascertain how many would be in for tea in case he should fill the pot too full. He collected the dirty mugs as he counted heads. We all had our own mugs, which was just as well as Joss's washing up was very random.

Eschewing an electric kettle – or maybe there was no power point nearby – he brewed up using an old tin kettle which he balanced precariously on a gas ring. This stood beside the metal pot that was used for melting blocks of fish glue, the stuff that was applied with a large bristle brush to stick up the bundles of newspapers for local delivery to newsagents and to slap on the direction labels. Somehow the tea so eagerly awaited always smelt strongly of fish.

But despite this, Bill our sub was a great tea drinker. In fact he was a great drinker, period, since most evenings he was to be found in a local hostelry cradling his tankard, but it did mean that he picked up a great many leads for stories. Bill had a special arrangement with Joss, that he, and he alone, had one cup in the morning during the editorial conference while a second, rapidly cooling one would be waiting for him on his desk upstairs.

I discovered after the first day that my tea drinking was curtailed on Mondays and Thursdays as it was my job to Meet the Bus. Bill had impressed upon me the importance of this task. He always spoke of it as a rite or ceremony and it duly gained upper case letters (and my initials beside it) in the bible. Bill had spent so many years composing headlines and using capital letters to make a point that he was apt to use this emphatic tone – certainly no adjectives – in his notes and everywhere.

What it actually meant was entirely undramatic. Someone had to Meet the Bus to collect parcels of advertisements from the sub-office run by one all-round member of staff in Princes Risborough. The parcel would also contain copy from local village correspondents on that bus route, and maybe reports of cricket or football matches for John to rewrite while the news reporters dealt with the WI reports or news from churches, clubs and schools.

It was another economy that the proprietor considered it cheaper to use the bus as a parcel conveyor rather than the Royal Mail, for he always feared things getting 'lost in the post', and spoke of the post office as if it were a branch of the Lost Property Office.

He was also very suspicious of the telephone and believed, as did the Editor, that reporters should be out on the job, as they had been in his young days. He would send staff miles to collect a small item of news when it would have been far simpler, quicker and possibly cheaper to have telephoned for the information.

I discovered that I was not to leave for the bus stop before the Editor arrived at 9.30am, so it was no good planning to pick up the parcel on the way to the office and so gain a little more time in bed. The bus was supposed to arrive at 9.45am, so I had ample time to get to the stop. But in winter the bus was nearly always late so tea was over by my return, and I didn't have the courage to get a cup at a café while still in charge of the precious parcel.

About once a fortnight, the bus would arrive early, and would already have gone on its way by the time I – and usually a number of irate passengers who were not best pleased to have missed it – arrived at the stop. The plan was that the bus conductor would take our parcel and any others to the nearby hardware shop, which had a large notice in its window that it acted as an agent for the bus company's collection and distribution of parcels. Once or twice it happened that the shop assistant mislaid our parcel, and it would be found lurking under a pile of something on the counter where the conductor had hastily flung it.

Then there was the crisis when it was carried on all the way to High Wycombe by a new conductor, and went missing despite God sending out what I could only think of in Bill's headline terms as a Special Messenger – a reporter on a bicycle trying to catch up with the bus. They couldn't trace the parcel at the bus terminus, but it turned up five or six hours later at Princes Risborough where it had first been placed on the bus, having done a tour of the county.

DAVE WAS detailed to show me the ropes on my first Monday. We were to go to the Market Square and discover what the strange thing on the top of the statue was, and to get the man from the photography shop in the square to take a picture of it. "This is your first assignment," Bill told me and handed me my first reporters' notebook, which was a thrill in itself.

I felt full of importance and longed to start out on my first 'story', however banal it sounded. Dave seemed intent on hanging around. Then I realised he was waiting for the tea. Because it was free and so grudgingly provided, I soon learned every reporter tended to do this and arrange the day so as not to miss it.

Dave initiated me in the daily calls I would carry out, but stressed that these must not be attempted until after the parcel was delivered to the Editor's hands. "It might contain a sensational scoop," he said with a wry smile, instead of a bundle of classified advertisements, so I was not to wander round with it.

He said a senior reporter went daily to the police station where the duty sergeant would provide details of any accidents or other incidents, and there was also a daily call to the fire station. Juniors cut their teeth on obituaries. My round would therefore start with visits to the three local undertakers.

I felt a bit like a puppy trailing around after Dave, trying to remember all the things he told me, but most of his conversation was about how rotten God was, how hard I would have to work for him, and how glad he was to be leaving.

"What are you going to do?" I asked, imagining him on his

way to Fleet Street after the rigorous training he'd received on the *Herald*, or at least to a job on an evening or daily in a big provincial city. But he explained that his ambitions were musical and not journalistic and that was why he and the paper were parting company. Dave was taking his trumpet to Margate for the summer season on the pier with a band. He had played all the previous winter with a local dance band, and consequently often fell asleep in the office, or overslept and arrived after God. Sometimes he had been forced to leave early from an evening meeting that he was covering in order to play at a dinner or early engagement with the band.

His landlady was unable to keep up with the unusual hours of his two careers, and gave up in despair. She would cook the lunch and supper to which he was entitled daily, and when he did not appear at the correct time would put the plate in the oven so that the meal could be hastily re-heated by Dave when he came in. He often had the choice of five or six plates of cold congealed stew and vegetables or limp fried fish, with the plates at the rear of the oven smelly and even growing mould.

God's patience had finally snapped the day before I had seen the advertisement for a reporter. Once more Dave had arrived mid-morning, and had been caught creeping past the Editor's office and making for the creaking stairs. God came out into the hallway so that the advertisement manager and printers working on the stone and the reporters upstairs could hear every word.

"You're late again, Dave," he snapped. "Overslept again I

suppose. I left the Hunt Ball early last night ready for a full day's work but I saw you still tootling away. I've told you before that I like reporters to have interests in the town. It all helps in getting the news, but playing in a dance band doesn't do anything for the image of the paper."

"Sir," replied Dave, as soon as he could get a word in, and he sounded most indignant to the listening reporters. "I did not oversleep. I started walking to work earlier than usual. But I was offered a lift, and I took it. It was one of the undertakers, and I thought I might pick up a name or two – but unfortunately I didn't realise that he was driving the hearse, and, out of respect for the coffin in the rear, our progress was slow and stately. Much slower than walking speed. With hindsight I should have got out and walked."

There was a muffled explosion of laughter from the listening audience, and it was immediately silenced by the stern voice of God making a decided pronouncement to a minor and erring angel – "You go at the end of the month and you take your trumpet with you."

So that was how I got the job of junior reporter. The other two men couldn't manage to cover everything, even though it was the start of the 'silly season' in mid-July and news was scarce. Len and Stan considered themselves too senior to attend to the chores the junior's work involved and, as family men, they had August holidays booked.

But on my first morning I knew none of this and believed I

had been chosen for the job from a long list of suitable applicants, not the first and only choice who could start immediately.

DAVE AND I finished our disgusting tea, left the office and made for the Market Square. I could see that half a loaf and a beer bottle were balanced on the bewigged head of John Hampden by the War Memorial. It made this seventeenth century worthy look so undignified that I started giggling. However, the pigeons were squabbling over the bread. It was obvious they would either peck it away or knock it down.

David gazed up too, and seemed in no hurry to call at the photographer's shop to ask Mr Haddock to take a photograph. We did employ a photographer – he and Joss were the only two with driving licences – but Michael, our photographer, refused to act as chauffeur for reporters if the job didn't entail taking pictures, and as it was he had to dash from place to place (and on Saturdays from wedding to wedding) to make all his assignments. So we employed Mr Haddock on a freelance basis.

He certainly lived up to his name. Mr Haddock was a keen naturalist and every week submitted photographs of wild life to Mr Godber, who usually returned them with a terse note asking why Mr Haddock had not taken a picture of the fire in the café opposite his shop, or the brick lorry which overturned and deposited its load on the pavement and road causing traffic chaos in the Market Square. "The trouble is he's got no news sense at all," Bill and the Editor would comment to each other as they

John Hampden without adornments: not an easy chap to climb.

shook their heads over yet another photograph of a robin's nest in an old flowerpot.

"I suppose," I said to Dave, "someone climbed up the statue last night and put the loaf and the bottle up there."

33

"As the clock struck midnight," Dave said solemnly. "It seemed quite funny then. But I can't think why Bill wants a story on it. He must have too much space this week."

Just then the quarrelling birds knocked both the loaf and the bottle off the statue, the bottle smashing on the plinth

"Thank goodness for that," said Dave. "I was wondering what we could cook up in the way of a story."

"Couldn't we have asked people who live around here if they saw or heard anything odd last evening," I asked. Wasn't that the way journalists got their facts?

"Trouble is they might have looked out of their bedroom windows and seen the culprit," Dave said seriously.

Then he took my arm. "I'll buy you a coffee if you promise not to tell," he said as he steered me towards the shabby looking transport café, the one that had recently had the fire Mr Haddock chose to ignore. When we were seated he looked over his shoulder to make sure no one could hear and whispered, "I put them there."

I giggled and managed to whisper back, "What were you going to do if someone had seen you and told Mr Godber?"

"I don't know." He shrugged his shoulders and stirred the sugar in the cup. "Last night when we came back from playing, I gave the old boy a short solo. Then we saw the bottle and the loaf in the gutter and the band bet me I wasn't sober enough to put them on the head. So I did it. And I can tell you he's not an easy chap to climb."

"You should go up again with something more permanent to mark your going."

"Perhaps – that's an idea. Sorry I'm not going to be around with you on the *Herald*. It should be a bit more lively."

And indeed so it was, in ways I had never dreamt.

– 2 –

PRESS GANG

THIS IS the century of the computerised everything, of instant worldwide communication and information via the internet, electronic mail and more. But in the early 1950s, even telephone communication was only available to a small percentage of the population, especially in rural areas. When I started work on the *Herald*, printing of the written word had hardly changed since the days of Caxton's moveable type nearly five hundred years earlier. Many of the newspaper's working practices and attitudes were just about as hoary, too.

At the rear of the premises was the old flatbed printing press where the heavy pages of type, locked up in their metal frames, were hoisted and manoeuvred into place by old Dick, the machine operator whose designer stubble was so far ahead of its time it was simply called scruffy, and the ever-grumbling Joss. The two of them also had to manhandle the enormous reels of newsprint into place with only a porter's barrow to help them.

The space in which the press reposed had been barely

adequate when it was installed sometime in the 1930s to replace a late Victorian press. But this second machine could only print a limited number of pages at one time, so an extension had been added. Thinking about it, I can see Joss actually had every reason for moaning as he did.

My first few weeks were hectic. I didn't really know whether I was doing the right thing or not and every new job brought more dramas and difficulties. Thank goodness for Pete. He was the oldest serving member of staff and liked to reminisce. "Of course things are so much simpler nowadays," he would say. "It's all so straightforward now."

It certainly didn't seem that way to me as I struggled with a pile of the 'reports' – I hesitate even now to demean that noble word – sent in by the public. There were jottings on the back of shopping lists, recycled envelopes, scraps of whatever paper was handy, every one of them (or so it seemed) written in pencil in a barely intelligible scrawl and missing some vital piece of information. In theory, all the reporters were supposed to rewrite a few of these gems during lulls in the main action. That was the theory anyway.

Pete found me sitting alone at the reporters' table, picking through a mound of these scribblings in the fading hope of finding one that made sense. "I'm heading down to the composing room," he said. "Would you like to see round the works and find out what happens to your work?" Good old Pete. I was out of my chair like a greyhound from its trap.

We went down from the first floor, bypassed the hallway – which was usually the only bit of the building where the public went – and made for the small door at the rear. Pete opened it and we stepped through to a small landing with a railing from which we could look down on the composing room with its big metal-topped block like an enormous table stretching from end to end. This I had to learn to call the 'stone'; I never could figure that one out when clearly it was a table.

The room was large, airy and clear, with vast skylights supported on cast iron brackets. It reminded me of Victorian railway stations, as well it might because it had been built the same way and probably at about the same time. Dangling above the stone was a row of electric lights in white enamel shades. All around the room were open-fronted wooden boxes fitted one above the other and at a slight angle to the walls so that letters of type could be tossed into the right one by the printers and their apprentices for re-use. When the headlines and cross-heads or the advertisements were being composed, the printers would move quickly from box to box with the ease of years of training to collect the right pieces of type which they assembled on a metal trough cradled on one arm. Choice words flew (usually at the apprentices) when a badly-aimed letter turned up in the wrong box, and the compositor had to break his concentration and rhythm to put it in its correct home and pluck another from the box.

On that particular quiet summer Monday afternoon, only the

foreman, a genial full-waisted man named Albert, and a couple of men, were working on the stone. "At one time we printed half the paper on a Tuesday, and the paper was put to bed much earlier on Thursdays than it is now," Pete explained from our vantage point. "If a lot of advertisements came in late, then the news had to suffer. All the dull stuff like the Women's Institute reports would make it every week, because they were submitted in time for the Tuesday print run. But the news planned into the other half of the paper would get bumped by the adverts. Unless it was news that could be carried over for a week to the next issue, it was spiked." He sighed, obviously pained by the memory of good stories impaled.

Just after the war, the *Herald's* circulation was going down rapidly as readers deserted it for our rival, the *Courier*. So the proprietor was persuaded to invest in an expensive extension to the old printing press. This was bolted on in what seemed a very Heath Robinson fashion, but it did mean we could print more pages at a time, and it also introduced automatic folding and cutting.

"Before that everyone had to help with folding the sheets and putting them in order," Pete explained. "Actually it wasn't too bad because with paper rationing during the war, we could only print a very small paper. As it's a broadsheet, we sometimes only had six pages, and one summer went down to one sheet of four because no one was taking large advertising space.

"But there were twice as many classifieds as now. Everyone wanted things that weren't on sale in the shops and anyone with something spare could be sure of getting rid of it for a good price. People who had been bombed out were glad of anything."

We went down the steps into the composing room proper. They showed me the metal frames on which the pages would be made up, the covered ink tray and its cumbersome roller which fitted across the stone and would ink the heavy pages so one or two proofs could be pulled before two apprentices carefully carried the frames through the Linotype room and into the print room.

Pete bent down and picked up a bar of silver metal from the floor. "Joss is as thorough as ever sweeping up, I see." He and Albert exchanged a look.

"It's called a slug," Albert told me. "It's a single line from a story – maybe one of yours." He cast his eye over what to me looked like gibberish, but he could read this upside-down, back-to-front language immediately, something I never learned to do. Albert popped the slug in the top pocket of his brown cotton overalls where it joined a couple of pencils, his pipe and reading glasses. All the printers wore these unflattering overalls; it gave them all a bosomy appearance.

Pete led the way around the stone to a door at the back of the room and into the Linotype room. There was only a small skylight overhead, but each of the three large Linotype machines had a built-in lamp by the operator's keyboard. Albert slid into the seat of the nearest machine; there was an immediate racket when he switched it on to give me a demonstration of how it worked.

The Linotype operator would clip our copy above the

keyboard and type it out again. As he typed, a series of brass letter moulds slid down a chute and collected in a small channel. When he reached the end of a line, he pulled a lever and liquid metal flowed over the moulds, forming a slug as it cooled. The slugs fed into another tray to create a column of type for the newspaper.

No one was working in the room that afternoon, but it was extremely noisy when all three machines were running later in the week. None of the operators wore ear-plugs, but they communicated with each other by lip-reading. There was obviously nothing wrong with their eyes; although the lighting in the room was quite dim, I could see its walls were decorated with the ubiquitous pin-ups.

We ignored a couple of other closed doors and walked through an open one to the print room. To call it claustrophobic would be too generous. The extension to the printing press left only inches between some of the walls and the moving parts of the press. The machine operator with his oil can and spanners had to be a contortionist to get at some bits of the press. The noise it made was thunderous; the whole building would shake as it roared into action. None of this would be tolerated – or legal – today, but back then, that's just the way it was.

I returned to my chair buoyed to think I was a link right at the beginning of a chain. Now that I knew what it was, the smell of printing ink that had gradually seeped into every corner of the building no longer concerned me, and the thud of the rollers on the flatbed was a sign that another edition of the paper was on its way. It was a comforting sound early on a Thursday evening that we had got another edition out.

Nothing was wasted: everyone still had the wartime mentality that resources were scarce. It wasn't just the proprietor wanting to save money: the staff recycled too. So when the paper that kept the enormous rolls of newsprint clean in transit was cut away after they were put in place, the youngest apprentice collected the sizeable pieces and cut them down to octavo size (just over a third of A4) on a big, vicious guillotine. This was what we used in our typewriters for copy paper.

At the end of the week, someone collected all the blacks (the carbon copies) which had been on the spikes in the Editor's room, and the originals from the reader's room, and put them on even bigger spikes. This was just in case there was a query about a story and blame could be attributed to the person who had made the mistake.

These lethal metal spikes came with a heavy wood base. When they filled up, the top would be bent over, dates inked on the top and bottom bits of paper, and then they were filed in the most basic fashion: they were hung on a row of hooks near the ceiling in the reader's room where they gathered the dust of years. I don't recall ever seeing any of them discarded... or consulted.

Everyone used spikes. It's a wonder there were so few skewerings. The two small and potentially lethal versions on our cluttered table held the detritus of the office such as letters containing invitations, the many items sent in by local correspondents, the basic information from which the cattle market reports or the flower shows had been written up. Theoretically these were spiked in date order to make it easier to check something. When our second spike was filled, which usually took a couple of months, we stripped the first of all its paper straight into the waste bin and started filling it up again. It was a straightforward and crude form of filing, but it seemed to work well. We were nearly always able to look up the right piece of paper if needed.

Towards the end of my time there, the office was modernised. The reporters' room and the subs office were amalgamated, and we got separate desks and a filing cabinet. After that it was impossible to find anything.

Almost anything. On a Friday morning, one item could always be found and that was the chief reporter's chips. He sent out for them when we worked late on a Thursday evening and if they weren't finished, he filed the newspaper-wrapped parcel in the top A-to-G drawer. On Friday mornings at 'elevenses' when we drank our 10am tea, he retrieved the package and ate cold chips. "Anyone?" he would say, offering the parcel. He got more verbal abuse than takers. If the tea always tasted of reeking fish, so everything filed in the top drawer of our new metal filing cabinet smelt of frying oil and stale chips.

The chips – or rather the package wrapping them – did give us a few laughs. The local chippy took our unsold papers to use as insulation on the hot chips, so we might find ourselves pulling a chip out from something we'd written weeks before. But they gave us a small discount in return for our papers, and in those days, every little bit helped.

FRIDAY MORNINGS were leisurely compared with the rest of the week, and theoretically reporters finished at noon with a half-day off. This was because we all worked in the office on Saturday mornings and mostly had jobs on Saturday afternoons ranging from sports to assorted church festivities. Sometimes those afternoons stretched into Saturday evenings, but often these jobs were dinners or dances and so more enjoyable.

But Friday morning was also the only time of the week when we were very tempted to write fiction. This was the weekly writing up of expenses; literary merit never entered the equation but I can't say the same of imagination. There was much head-scratching as we tried to remember, with the help of the bible, where we had been. Most of our expense claims were for reimbursement of bus or train fares, but if we had not been able to get home between leaving work and an evening job, we were allowed to claim a very small amount for a meal. Of course, if you knew in advance, you could bring sandwiches and cake to eat at your desk, and look forward to a bit more untaxed money in your pay packet.

Bus fares offered another window of creative opportunity. By getting off at an early stop and walking to the job – always assuming there was time – I could claim the few pence more involved in taking the bus from door to door. If the journey was local, I could walk or use the office bicycle, so sometimes I was claiming for a non-existent bus trip.

Another wheeze was to claim for two single fares although you had purchased the cheaper return ticket. These entries only netted any of us a shilling or two extra a week, but what amounts to small change today made a difference back then.

Unfortunately there was a sudden clamp-down from the accounts department of the printing works office up the road, where the wages were paid. Henceforth and with immediate effect, we would have to attach the actual tickets to the expenses forms to get reimbursed.

We were indignant. Cheat on expenses – us? Why, the very suggestion verged on slander. So another cat-and-mouse game began. We got in the habit of picking up bus tickets from the floor of the vehicle just in case they could be used at a later date.

THE ONE fiddle still on my conscience, after more than half a century, is travelling on the train without a ticket. I suppose I could argue I was forced into it by circumstances.

There was one parish council that met in the evening in a very small village called Kimble which still had a railway halt in the days of steam trains and before Dr Beeching's cuts removed nearly all the country rail lines. It was possible to get there on the bus, and this was considerably cheaper and quicker than the train, but the last bus home left before the meeting started, so there was really no alternative but to catch the final train of the night back. The thing was, the Kimble halt was unmanned in the evenings. When the sole employee – ticket issuer, porter, flag waver and grower of magnificent red geraniums – left for his tea after the six o'clock commuter train had chuffed busily out of the station, he would leave a lit oil lamp on the edge of the single platform. To get the last train to stop, you stood on the platform and strained your senses to glimpse the puff of smoke in the distance and hear the sound of the train approaching.

In the summer, this was fine because the train driver and his stoker would see anyone who was waiting and stop. But the method on dark winter nights was to lift the paraffin-fuelled lantern high and swing it about – not too hard or you'd put it out – hoping and hoping that the driver was on the lookout and would stop. British Railways had recently been nationalised, and it was the only time I really felt that the railways belonged to me, as well as the rest of the country, when I could lift a lantern and stop the train just for myself.

The train was always made up of one or two of the old carriages that didn't have a corridor, and conveniently there was also no guard's van, and hence no guard. So once the train had stopped, the stoker got down from the engine cab and extinguished the lantern while I hopped into the nearest carriage. I was usually was the sole passenger back to the mainline station. It felt like royalty having one's own train, although it was filthy dirty with torn seats, a littered floor and no heating.

Making the journey that way meant there was no-one to issue me with a ticket at the halt, and no inspector on the train to check it. The ticket office at the mainline station would be closed for the night as there were no more stopping trains until the 'milk train' left for London in the early hours of the morning, so there was no way of paying for a ticket on arrival.

So every so often I could claim the train fare knowing I wouldn't have my expenses form flung back at me because my ticket wasn't clipped to it, because everyone knew tickets were always collected by the man at the station.

And how much did this misdemeanour earn me? A princely half a crown in pre-decimal money – about twelve and a half pence in today's coinage. It pales into insignificance against the expenses claimed by MPs and businessmen.

THE KIMBLE stationmaster was a kindly man who quite enjoyed what looked to me like a fairly undemanding job. Such were his duties that he had time to make the derelict space opposite the platform into his own vegetable garden. He grew plenty of flowers too. He regularly won prizes in the local horticultural shows.

He was from the old school and looked after his passengers well, treating them as friends rather than travellers or customers. On cold winter mornings, the city gents arrived in their pin-striped suits and bowler hats, carrying furled umbrellas. Many wore wellingtons or galoshes on their feet, and serviceable but unfashionable mackintosh capes and coats. Most walked to the station, although a few were driven by wives; not many people owned two cars, and there was no car park at the little station, just a lay-by on the country road outside.

The stationmaster had a coal fire in his ticket office so everyone could wait in comfort. When they got on the train, they would pass their boots back to him, and he would obligingly put them to dry in the office ready for his owners' return in the evening. The city gents would take their lace-up black or brown shoes, polished to a mirror finish, from their pockets or brief cases and don them for the journey.

One unforgettable day, a commuter known for cutting things fine had been in even more of a dash than usual to get the 6.30am train. He handed over his wellingtons and his thick tweed Ulster overcoat, and sat back in his corner seat to get his newspaper out of his brief case and as the train steamed out the station, he realised that he had forgotten to pack his shoes. Apparently his socks were worn to holes and his feet black and sore before he reached the end of Paddington Station and was able to get a taxi and wait for a shoe shop to open. A reader submitted that story – though whether thoughtfully of gleefully we couldn't decide. We spiked it, of course, but only after it had been circulated throughout the office.

WITH THE management's Shylock mentality to expenses, it was only to be expected that the clerk from the printing office who brought us our pay packets would arrive at one minute to noon (the time we began our half-day). No-one would leave early without our brown envelopes full of cash.

It was the same for the printers. Friday was their 'dissing' day, when they dissembled the pages. The headlines in those days were still created letter by letter out of reusable type. Those pieces of type, as well as the used lead slugs, had to be recovered. On Friday, the printers unbolted the pages and dismantled them on the big stone in the print room. Starting with the big fonts, they tossed individual letters of different print faces and sizes into the open-mouthed wooden boxes which lined the room in several tiers. They 'minded their Ps and Qs' with unerring accuracy as letters rained down into the various boxes whose labels had long since become illegible and torn. The Linotype slugs were collected to be melted back down so that the recycled metal would form the print face for the next week's paper. The leads used to separate the columns went back into their places.

With the 'dissing' done, the printers waited impatiently for their wage packets. Since noon was also the time the pubs around the market square opened, they could go off to buy their pints and vanish until Monday or Tuesday morning.

ALTHOUGH WE operated far from the big dailies in Fleet Street, the printers' union had a stranglehold on our printers. The Father of the Chapel, a.k.a. the Shop Steward, was Albert, the foreman, so when he gave orders, he expected everybody to obey.

Although his authority technically covered only the printers, he could if he wished disrupt the entire process.

I had been told almost on the first day working on the paper that on no account was I ever to handle or touch a piece of type. Only printers were allowed to do this. The sub and the Editor could go down and stand by the stone as the production of the paper progressed, but they could only point to anything they wanted to change, and tell the foreman. He in turn told one of the printers while the apprentices stood by and watched (and learned). The piece of type would be moved or changed, and then the printer told the foreman what he had done, and he told the journalist. Although everyone in the room knew what was happening without this elaborate pantomime, these were the cast iron rules of a closed shop.

Bill smoked in the works. One day, the foreman by his shoulder, he leaned over the stone to point out something he wanted the printer to change. All should have been straightforward as usual – but the long sausage of ash dropped off Bill's cigarette and landed squarely on the black, glistening and newly inked page of type. It would have been simple for the foreman to have blown it off, or maybe flipped it off with a cloth. But the ash belonged to a journalist, so was technically part of a journalist, and the journalist was forbidden to touch the type. "Just flick it off," said Bill. "Oh no, can't do that," replied Albert with much tutting and sucking of teeth.

Things were getting a bit fraught with tempers starting to fray and accusations bouncing to and fro. The foreman threatened to call an immediate strike of all printers if anyone but him touched the type, and he was not going to touch it as it wasn't ash from his cigarette. That week's edition was in jeopardy.

Bill and Albert stormed into God's office to continue their argument. The foreman was going to telephone his union office, and get a ruling. Bill was all for forbidding the use of the office phone and making the foreman go to the public telephone kiosk. "We can have rules too," he growled. "What will the National Union of Journalists say if we let a printer use our phone?" He had conveniently forgotten that the phone belonged to the owners of the print works, not the NUJ, but it must have seemed a good counterpunch at the time.

Luckily Joss arrived with tea, and Bill had to go upstairs to his room to fetch his packet of cigarettes, so Albert made the phone call hastily in his absence. I don't know what the official verdict was, because by the time the three of them had drunk their tea, and trooped back into the print room, some young apprentice (who was not yet a union member) had wiped the offending ash off. No evidence, no crime: everyone pretended the incident had not happened and carried on putting a paper to bed.

Smoking was banned in the basement printing area and even Bill, who somehow had blagged an exemption to the rule, stopped after that day. But one odd rule, which the print union had passed and which was observed in our works, was that once the printers were on overtime, they were allowed to smoke.

A pointless little war waged between the management who didn't want to pay out the extra money, and the printers who objected to being rushed if there was more work to be done. There was a large clock in the composing room and when it reached five – which was their knocking off time on Mondays to Wednesdays – Bert, the foreman, would produce his pipe and one or two of the others would light cigarettes. But on Thursdays, when they all had to work late and under pressure, somehow no one smoked and everyone got on with the job.

It wasn't just union rules that made the printers an arrogant elite. They had all been apprentices at one time and spent years learning their craft. All were proud of their abilities both in working the Linotype machines at speed and in setting the type and knew that they were highly skilled craftsmen who could get good jobs anywhere. All of them had been with the *Herald* for years, and took a pride in producing a paper with no errors, every line straight and square and every page looking as it should. They were as loyal to the firm as were we in the editorial department.

THERE WERE other dramas with the print department because the printing press operator, Bert, was also a volunteer fireman, and had roped in two of his colleagues. The town's full-time fire crew always went out first; we could hear the clanging bell as the fire engine rushed down the street. But if they had to phone for backup, the works siren at the Bif was sounded, so that all the volunteer firemen who heard it would drop everything and dash to the central fire station until they had enough to form a crew and the standby engine could go off to the fire.

In our printing works, the men were eager to attend the fire because it was more cash and their wages at their job would not be stopped. Often with inky hands, they would rush to the yard for their bikes and pedal off rapidly, leaving whatever they had been doing. If we heard the siren at any but the regular times, we knew Bert would be off and probably the other two as well, reducing the printing work force by half at a stroke. Of course it also meant the paper could often print a much better report on the fire than the official one given out at the fire station. Bert could provide more details and give the routine account some excitement, but it was very awkward to lose half the staff on a day when the paper was about to be printed and not know when they would return.

It wasn't one of our printers but another very keen volunteer fireman who made the front page of our paper for another reason. This chap was always the first to reach the fire station, flinging aside his bike and rushing into his uniform to be on the first volunteer engine to go out. Unfortunately he was also an arsonist, so it emerged, and it was fires he had set that he went back to douse.

One Friday morning, there was a huddle of printers in the hall waiting to see God. Bill and Pete were also called in and at tea time that morning, we all attended a meeting in the reporters' room with Michael and the reader and his boy.

"Not a word of this to anyone," Bill said sternly.

It appears the arsonist had turned up to the fire station ready to fight a fire that he had set – but had forgotten to make his usual telephone call to report the fire and call out the regular engine! We couldn't have suppressed it even if we'd wanted because the case came up at the Magistrates' Court the following week.

I NEVER GOT quite as lazy a half-day on the Friday morning as the more senior reporters. True, there was no Meeting the Bus, and the undertakers had to wait until Monday for my visit, but Friday morning was reserved for the particular purgatory known as writing up the week after next week's cinema programmes.

Unless they had a really popular film, both the local cinemas had a change of programme mid-week and also showed old films on Sundays. Since all the programmes consisted of a 'B' film before the main feature, I had to get details of eight films. The managers provided small sheets giving the titles and the stars, and sometimes there would be a short synopsis of the story. With the 'B' features, this information was often missing or not available two weeks in advance, so I would have a short discussion with the managers, who were helpful in looking through their trade literature to discover what the film was about, or if any of those in it would be names recognised by filmgoers.

"Do you think *Away in the West* would be a Western, with cowboys?" I asked when we could find nothing about the film.

The manager frowned. "You'll have to write that the

supporting film is *Away in the West*," he said. "We can't make assumptions just on the title."

Unfortunately that wouldn't fill the space I had been allotted since I had to write the same amount of editorial for each of the cinemas because they both paid for the same-sized advertisement each week and would complain to God if I gave one more column-inches than the other. Personally, I thought most people went to the pictures at least once a week anyway, and would see the trailers for the next week's attractions. And anyway, they could go and look at the posters outside if they didn't know what was on. But to cover myself I usually wrote something like *Away in the West* was a film not to be missed.

The blockbuster films with famous stars always sold out and often there were long queues for seats. That explained why some people went early to get a seat even if they had to sit through a poor 'B' film.

If the Aylesbury cinemas were a chore, the three small cinemas in nearby towns which also advertised with the *Herald* were a trial. I would telephone their managers, but usually got no answer, so I had to go downstairs to the advertisement office to see if their copy had arrived. If it had, all was well because they always had films some weeks or even months after they had been shown on the main circuit in town. It was then just a question of looking back through the files for the information on these films when they were first shown, and getting their write-ups done and out of the way. They got fewer words anyway.

The only good thing about writing up the films was that I was able to use the free pass which both of the main cinemas issued to the paper. These passes were only supposed to be used once a week and each admitted two people. But by dint of 'forgetting' to give the passes back to God, we could share them around between the younger reporters – and occasionally the printers too.

I found that the passes were popular with whatever boyfriend had asked me to go to the pictures – about the only entertainment there was. But usually my dates had been put off much earlier because of the fact that I had to work so often in the evenings, as well as nearly every Saturday afternoon and sometimes Saturday evenings.

Occasionally work could be combined with pleasure. The younger reporters, including me, were always eager to cover the meetings of the Young Conservatives. Not that we had any particular political leanings, but the meetings attracted young, unattached men and there was a good social programme too. So sitting through a dreary lecture on something like 'What the budget means for you' could lead to an invitation to the next dance or outing.

For the same reason, I also went to numerous meetings of various of the local Young Farmers' Club where it seemed that learning about the latest trends in agriculture ran a poor second to meeting other farmers' daughters and the occasional outsider like myself. I lost count of the number of boring and incomprehensible talks I sat through and judging by the roving eyes of the young farmers also in the room, I wasn't alone. There was always a stampede for the coffee and home-made cakes after the meeting when, in the more informal atmosphere, we could chat and possibly get a date.

THE IDEA of getting as much of the routine copy written on Friday and Saturday mornings was so that great wodges would be ready for the Linotype operators on Mondays and the galley proofs ready to go upstairs to the reader's room. The reader's boy was always being sent down to collect these proofs, which were rolled around the reporters' copy. He usually collected them before the ink was dry, so the copy and the galley was always smudged and difficult to read, as were his hands and face by the end of his shift.

We reporters found that by getting these reports out of the way, we could start writing up our Saturday jobs when we got into the office on Mondays. That was why I was assailed by so much bashing of typewriters on my first Monday, and why I was soon contributing to the cacophony.

COMPETITION between newspapers meant owners and editors were always looking for new ways of attracting advertising revenue. Our great rival, the *Courier*, was part of a chain and printed on a much more modern press in Luton. One autumn we noticed it was printing bigger issues and getting more advertising. We weren't keeping up and needed to do something. Our owner,

God and Mr Carruthers, the advertisement manager, went into conference. Then one Saturday morning at the beginning of November, everyone was called to a meeting in God's office. On one side of the room, the editorial staff grouped together, suspiciously eying the printers on the other and the photographer, the blockmaker, the reader and the reader's boy hovered in between, with Joss.

"We have to do something to get circulation moving up," announced Mr Godber, with the advertisement manager and the owner flanking him. "We're going to make this happen with a special type of Christmas advertising."

What Mr Carruthers would promise to all those paying for an advertisement was that they would be featured in a short piece of editorial in a special section of the news part of the paper. The editorial staff would write this, and the length of each piece would be appropriate to the amount of space the advertiser had taken.

Len and I were to take on this task, and Pete would see that we did not get diary jobs during the day – in effect everyone was going to do far more work for the same pay. As a female, I had most of the shops. The idea was that I could write about their stock, and suggest how excellent it was for Christmas presents.

This was fine for gift shops and even food shops, but then the local skip firm took a quarter page. Skips – would you like one for Christmas? I had used up almost all my ingenuity with hardware shops or painting and decorating stores and hoped that no one was going to blame me personally if their Christmas stockings contained pots of paint or wallpaper samples as a very heavy hint of what was expected. But giving this firm the same sort of write-up called for a different magnitude of 'creativity'.

At the end of the first week of this new regime, we were called to another meeting. The take-up on the advertising had been tremendous, said a pink and beaming Mr Carruthers. All the businesses were keen to have their write-ups in the main part of the paper.

But there was a down side. Because of demand for space, we would be printing an additional four or more pages a week – which would have to be inserted by hand, copy by copy, because our press couldn't print and gather a bigger issue. As the old hand who had done this job before, Pete had to give us a short pep talk on how simple it all was if it was organised properly. There was a growing swell of muttered discontent until we heard the owner say, "You can volunteer to help and if you do, you'll be paid overtime." This sop was enough to make everyone willing to take part except John, the sports editor, who had the problem of getting home to his village. No one could expect lifts in the van because that would be busy delivering papers.

So the first week of the new regime began. On the Tuesday, the early pages were printed as usual. On the Wednesday, the Christmas advertising edition with its columns of articles for the advertisers joined them, stacked in great teetering piles in the Linotype room ready for insertion into the main paper on Thursday evening. As usual, Thursday was a mad rush of getting late stories into print, proofreading, setting up pages, writing a strong front-page lead and eye-catching splash headline. Then, with some trepidation – because no-one knew how long it would take to insert the supplement into nearly thirty thousand copies – we made ready for our extra duties.

With the military precision of an old Home Guard member, God had worked out our positions. I was in his office where he would work on his desk, and I had a wobbly trestle table that had arrived from the main printing works up the road. The big table in the reporters' room had been cleared so that Len and Stan were standing ready while Pete and Bill were on duty in the subs room. The reader had also cleared his table and we all awaited the first copies.

The reader's boy and young apprentices came round with piles of the inserts and we put them on our desks. The Linotype operators and some of the young printers acted as runners. As the main paper came off the press, they formed a human chain to pass copies into the main building and up the narrow stairs.

The sheer number of papers overwhelmed us. It was backbreaking work to open each copy of the broadsheet evenly, trying not to smudge the print, and carefully push the insert into position. It had to be aligned exactly so that the paper could be folded again and then put on the finished pile, which grew inexorably until it threatened to crash down and urgent cries summoned a runner to come and take the papers away.

But there was equal confusion and muddle in the basement

where Joss and Bert were counting piles of finished papers, and putting them into bundles for distribution. And beneath all this was the heavy thump of the flatbed churning out more and more pages. Suddenly there was silence. The reel of paper was empty, and another had to be manoeuvred into its place. Then the thumping noise started all over again.

Gradually order was restored. The piles of papers were sorted better, and at last there was time to join the queue for the only lavatory, or to open sandwiches and thermos flasks of tea. It was after 2am when the last paper got its insert and we could go home.

The next day, everyone managed to get to work (well, it was payday), and surprisingly the whole team continued this work for six more weeks until Christmas. Thankfully, the following year, we were better organised and it was never quite such a mammoth task again.

WRITING THE various Christmas articles was actually quite good fun. I enjoyed visiting the different shops and businesses instead of making my regular rounds of the undertakers and the village news. But the man who advertised his skip hire business for Christmas did challenge my imagination and writing skills.

I found him down a back street; parked in the road was an old, rusty lorry with one bucket skip on the back. The office of the firm was the untidy front room of a house. A pile of papers on a table seemed to comprise the business part of the company. What could I write about this firm to help it get more business, and skate round the fact that it would not be the skip hire that I would choose? It looked to me to be doomed from the start, but the owner had paid for an advertisement in our Christmas supplement and somehow I had to write two hundred words suggesting that the public should patronise it without actually being libellous and misleading.

The unshaven and rather unsavoury owner came from upstairs after his wife shouted that "the girl from the paper" was there to see him. They both sat on the sagging settee while I perched on an armchair which had obviously just been vacated by the old Alsatian lurking by the door. "Do you employ anyone?" was the first question I could think of.

"Well, my brother and brother-in-law," he replied. "But you can't put that in the paper because they're both on the social and so I just give them cash. My wife sorts out the bills and that, so I don't need to pay her."

Obviously I needed a more devious approach. "Have you ever found anything unusual or interesting in your skip when you went to collect it?"

"Yes," he said. "Once there were some paintings and the frames were a bit broken. But you can't write about them because I took them to the local auction house and they sold for quite a bit. I know they're mine once they are in the tip, but if the owner read your bit he might come for a cut of the cash."

"Shall I say you offer a cheap and efficient service?" I suggested. What it had to do with Christmas and presents I could not work out, but at east it was inoffensive. After a few more minutes, I got up to go. "Thank you, Mr Smith. I can't promise which edition of the paper it will be in, but certainly before Christmas and in the same issue as your advertisement."

"Don't call me Mr Smith," he retorted. "No-one does. Everyone round here knows me as Pick-It-Up Pete – the name's Pete Smith."

That was the inspiration I had been looking for. As soon as I got back to the office, I sat down and wrote: 'For a whole lot of rubbish you want to get rid of before Christmas, just call for Pick-It-Up Pete,' and the rest followed easily. I wondered why he hadn't thought of calling his firm Pick-It-Up Pete's instead of North Street Skip Hire, but maybe it hadn't occurred to him that a catchy name would attract business even if a small doubt might cross the client's mind when the old lorry drove up.

Pete was kind enough to send a garish Christmas card to the office. It was one of those cards caked with glitter that got everywhere – we were still trying to get it off our copy in January. The card was signed from Pete, who added that my article had meant his phone hadn't stopped ringing and he couldn't keep up with the work. Anytime I was in his area I was welcome to call in and see him and his wife. But I never took up the invitation – the Alsatian hairs took nearly as long to get off my clothes as the glitter.

– 3 –

DEATH DUTIES

ONE OF the casualties – collateral damage, I suppose you'd call it – of the demise of local paid-for newspapers is the obituary. There's so much advertising in today's free local newspapers that the art of obituary writing – and it was an art, by which all cub reporters learnt their trade – has quite literally died out. Now the lives of the recently departed great and good usually appear only in national broadsheets. Young journalists of today with college training and often a degree are too expensive a commodity for a chief reporter to send them door-knocking for a paragraph or two on the demise of a common man or woman. But this was how I, and all young reporters in the area, started to learn their job.

Weddings and deaths were a staple feature or our weekly and thousands of others throughout the country. Newsprint had only recently been taken off ration, and at the *Herald*, suddenly God found he had to fill a greatly enlarged 'news hole' with items of interest if advertisements (and the way the paper made a profit) were not to be turned away. By law, newspapers had to carry a certain percentage of news to paid advertising, and 'free puffs', which now find their way into all printed matter via spin and publicity officers, were frowned upon – and quite rightly – by the old traditional newsmen.

So, early on my first day, after the story of the bottle and the bread on the statue had literally fallen down, Dave took me on a tour of the three local undertakers. They were always happy to provide a list of names of the dear departed because at the foot of each obituary the paper printed, in very small type, 'Funeral arrangements by so and so'. This slightly macabre way of advertising was a legitimate puff. I discovered that they appeared to run a kind of popularity stakes, and would greet me with the words, "We had a lot of business last week; see if you can get all these in print."

One particularly cold, wet winter day, as I sat shivering in the office of William Black and Son in front of a small coal fire, Mr Black (such an appropriate name for an undertaker) explained in all seriousness that "this awful weather has meant at very good week" for business. "There's probably more to come," he added, with quiet satisfaction, and I could almost see Uriah Heep wringing his hands in gleeful anticipation of profits rising as the temperature fell.

"A good many of those standing in freezing churchyards in their best funeral blacks rather than warmly wrapped up in their winter woollies are taking 'grave' risks," he added without the slightest trace of irony.

Did he chuckle with glee? Not exactly, but I imagined the thought of the extra business and the profit it would bring warmed him more than his miserly coal fire. But of course there was no guarantee that he would get the order instead of one of the other two. All three advertised their services, but they could hardly claim to be better or cheaper as most other commercial firms did.

Black and Son ran both a funeral parlour and a monumental masons business, together with a general carpentry firm. Although Mr Black Sr was supposed to have retired, he came into the works every day to find fault with Mr Black Jr. But he did still help out in periods like that cold snap.

One summer he took me through the carpentry workshop to a storage room at the back. There, under a dustsheet, was a pristine coffin. The wood and handles had been chosen with care; he had worked on it for many hours and completed it some time before. "It's for me," he said. As I stood there trying to think of something to say, he grabbed a duster from the shelf and gave it an extra polish. "All ready and waiting," he commented with pride, to all appearances oblivious to the irony that he would not be around to see the coffin actually in use.

ALL THREE undertakers could get annoyed with me on occasion. Usually it had to do with how many column inches each one got. It might happen that the biggest one had given me several names on the Monday morning, but only one obituary had found its way into the following issue of the *Herald*. His rivals, who had acquired fewer clients, had had their names mentioned several times at the end of each obituary. It was useless for me to explain that some families had not wanted anything in the paper, or others appeared to have gone away and their neighbours had no idea where. In fact it was in my own interest to get as many obituaries written as possible. The *Herald* paid a small commission for obtaining an announcement of the death, funeral service and a notice of thanks from the family in the appropriate classified columns. Many of those I met liked me to draft the wording, and soon I knew all the trite phrases that gave obits a style all their own. The families seemed to find this service most helpful.

However, there was a much more significant amount of commission to be earned if the relatives of the deceased could be persuaded to have a list of wreaths and their inscriptions printed. These would go immediately after the obituary and details of the funeral and just before the name of the undertakers. With my rock bottom wages, it was welcome extra cash even if it was earned in what seemed to me a rather unsavoury way.

Long lists of mourners – or indeed any lists of names – were a headache. Despite the decline of the class system, the one place where rank and privilege were alive and standing smartly to attention seemed to be the media. This meant that if you made a mistake in what was a very rigid order of precedence, someone was sure to give God earache.

Titles were easy enough: we consulted Debretts and learned

that dukes came first – not that we had any locally. After that came the earls and counts in descending order of importance, with barts and sirs bringing up the rear before the mere men and women made their appearance in roughly alphabetical order. Our reference books got a good thumbing; there was no Googling or getting the word processor to do the hard work.

Ranks in the services were, if anything, trickier. We had colonels, brigadiers and captains, all retired after the First World War with rank, which they were punctilious in still using. Even the ex-Home Guard used their former ranks.

As if that wasn't bad enough, the clergy was another minefield. Good old *Crockford's Clerical Directory* gave us the right terms to use for bishops and canons, archdeacons and deacons down to rectors and vicars, and ending with curates. At least they were always men then. Thank goodness we were spared the particular hell of using post-nominal letters – the degrees, fellowships, honours and so on people accumulate like barnacles through a long life.

EVERY MONDAY morning, having Met the Bus, delivered the packet, and then walked to the offices of the three undertakers, it was back to the office with my list. Pete looked it over. He had encyclopaedic knowledge of local bigwigs. If anyone famous in our locality had died, a senior reporter would write that person's obituary.

Occasionally a relative would volunteer to write something

and bring it to the office. That might have meant I lost a tiny commission on the death notice and the notice of thanks, but my legs would benefit with the respite from the long walks I took in every direction of our town chasing up addresses on my list. Sometimes I could borrow the office bicycle, but with rules on how women reporters should dress, cycling was only possible in fine weather.

If someone notable had died, it was my job to go and look them up in our Morgue. This was our name for another filing system where we could check what the paper had carried previously on that person. It was just a series of alphabetically arranged envelopes contained clippings from past issues – a golden wedding, a councillor's election, or perhaps a retirement and presentation – that could provide enough personal information for the basis of an obituary.

In the dull newsless days of late summer, the junior reporter spent time sifting through the envelopes to update the information on prominent individuals and to write up obituaries, just leaving space for the date of death, and even the cause in case it was an accident. This meant that should anyone notable be inconsiderate enough to die just before the print deadline with no time for an interview with the family, friends or colleagues, then the death could still be reported quite fully and the details fleshed out the following week, probably with the funeral report as well.

Taking the cuttings was the responsibility of the reader and the boy who was his copyholder. Usually the lad who took this position did so under the illusion that he would progress to a junior reporter. But Roy, the incumbent when I joined, had only been in the job a couple of months when he got his call-up papers for National Service, and so he would soon be leaving – though his job would be kept open for him to return to at the end of two years. But what twenty year old would chose to be closely closeted every day with a grumpy old man, and forced to read aloud pages of copy for checking? This was another obvious reason why I had been appointed as a junior reporter, but ignorance had been bliss, and not knowing all these facts, I believed I had obtained the job on merit.

Mr Smith, the reader, hated making the cuttings. He was supposed to do it on Saturday or Monday mornings when very little copy was coming through for him and Roy to check. Although he had a word-by-word knowledge of every item in each week's paper, having had to read it though at least twice, he suddenly became ignorant of the contents when Saturdays and Mondays came, so what was cut out and kept in the cuttings library was very hit and miss.

Ingenuity knew no bounds on those dull afternoons at the beginning of the week in the summer. Pete gave us a list of local dignitaries to phone (those who were on the telephone) and, using the pretext that we hoped to run a series on town or village personalities, pump them for enough information to form the basis of an obituary. When the stories failed to appear, God would be forced to plead pressure of space when meeting the likes of the mayor who thought he was going to get several columns on himself in an issue of the paper following the phone call. One did not like to point out that unfortunately he would never get the read the article, but like the Boy Scouts, it was a good idea to be prepared.

FOR THE most part, we knocked on doors. These were the homes of people in mourning. It was not fun. Fortunately there was a magic formula which nearly always got me entrance to the home of the deceased or the address the undertaker had given me. It was always a gamble because it was seldom I could telephone in advance and make an appointment. My first sentence was, "I'm a reporter from the *Herald* and we're sorry to hear of the death of Mr or Mrs or Miss Wotsit but we would like a few details about him/her to put in our next edition."

If I wasn't ushered across the doorstep immediately, or a slight hesitation was apparent, I followed up quickly by looking at the person and guessing which of the following two sentences would be the most appropriate:

"I believe he (or she) was very well liked and known in the area."

Or else, "It won't cost you anything."

One or the other, but especially the second phrase, always seemed to work. It was in fact very rare that I would be turned away.

On that first Monday morning, when Dave was showing me the ropes, this was part of what he covered. "Boring but widely read," was his assessment. "Some people turn to the obits first, even before they look at front page."

As we approached the first house, Dave said he'd ask the paper's stock questions and both of us would write down the replies. Then we would be able to check the accuracy between us. We knocked on the door of a small terraced house where, in the middle of the morning, all the curtains were drawn across the windows. I was terrified.

A small, cheerful-looking woman answered the door, and immediately led us into the back kitchen when we said that we were from the paper. This room was cheerful compared with the dark corridor of the hall and the glimpse we caught of the dim front parlour as we passed by the open door. She offered us tea and Dave started his interview.

The woman was very chatty, and Dave had difficulty keeping her to the point and getting the facts we wanted rather than a string of reminiscences. "It's a relief now he's dead," she commented as she showed us out. "He was ill for so long, and now I can go and live with my sister. We arranged it weeks ago."

As we approached the second house after a long walk through the town, Dave said without warning, "You do this one." I must have looked frightened, because he added, "I'll prompt you if you forget to ask anything. I can do obits in a trance."

This time it was a harassed-looking daughter who answered

the door. She told us that she was expecting the man about the insurance and was clearly disappointed we were not him. She didn't offer us tea and spent most of the time we were there looking out of the front room window at the street. Dave had now either gone into his famous trance or was catching up on the sleep he missed the previous night. Anyway, he wasn't monitoring my questions. As soon as we heard footsteps on the path, the daughter gave up and hustled us out of the house. She was hoping that the insurance agent would be able to pay out for the funeral expenses immediately, and then she could get on with clearing the house. I was hoping that I had remembered all the questions I was supposed to ask and had not forgotten anything vital.

After lunch – in Dave's case a liquid one as he had a lot goodbyes to make – we met up again at the office. Dave began to write up the first obituary on the one available typewriter, while I studied my shorthand notes and wondered how to turn them into a report.

"You've always got to do a black," he commented – that's what we called a carbon copy. "The black stays with the sub and then goes on to God so what you write can be checked back – so don't forget and don't put the carbon paper in back to front like I normally do and have to type the whole thing again because it's come out backwards on the front sheet and the black copy is a blank!"

The blacks would get greyer and fainter as the week wore on and the same carbon paper got fed through the roller for the umpteenth time because a new supply didn't get issued until Monday. You had to hit the keys of the heavy manual typewriters hard in order to make contact with the paper and produce a legible black. If you typed too fast, the keys had a tendency to stick together and the old ribbons to jump out of their restraining clips. What a carry-on.

Dave showed me how every piece of copy had to have a catch line that was repeated on page two and any subsequent pages so that the whole story stayed together if various pages were given to different Linotype operators. It was also essential to put my initials on the top of the story – again so either the sub or the Editor would know who to blame if something was wrong.

When he'd finished, I looked at what Dave had written. It was very short considering how long we had sat drinking tea and listening to the cheerful widow's stories. "Aren't you going to put in the bit about his war service?" I asked innocently.

Dave shook his head. "She couldn't remember where he was stationed in England, or his regiment, or the dates, so I've just written that he was in the army as a conscript during part of the Second World War."

"But what about that story of how he was in the lorry with the unexploded bomb and they dumped it, and she thought he and the others ought to have had a medal for bravery?"

"Bill would only cut that," he explained. "It's hearsay. Or if Bill let it go, God would call me into his office, demand an elaboration and then send me back to the house to get precise dates and details – and we know she'll probably be gone by now. It's a waste of time to write about it."

He looked at me and said solemnly, "First rule of the sub and the Editor to the reporter on a news story is: 'When in doubt – find out.' But take it from a disillusioned hack like me that the better mantra is: 'When in doubt – leave it out.'"

It took a few weeks but eventually I found that Dave was right and I could save myself a lot of angst and worry using his method.

There was a strict formula for writing obituaries, and any attempt at variation brought the sub-editor's blue pencil into action. The first paragraph gave the name, age, address and occupation of the deceased. The next listed any organisations he or she belonged to, plus possibly another couple of interesting facts. The third paragraph gave the names of the immediate family and details of the funeral service.

Any flights of literary prose were always heavily scored through and earned a rebuke. "You must write in the style of the *Herald*," God always emphasised to me. "You are not a fiction writer; we only want the facts. And never write a book about anything. Short and concise; keep it short and concise and absolutely correct."

If a reporter went to the funeral – as we did at least once a week – then there would be a long list of the mourners who attended the service, and even the wreaths and their inscriptions, though by that point in the story, the size of the font had diminished to minuscule. The final paragraph always named the undertaker. The editorial thinking behind this way of writing an obituary was that there was far less likelihood of getting the facts wrong facts or misinterpreting the information. God lived in fear that somehow the deceased and the family might be libelled.

Readers took particular delight in pointing out printing errors in obituaries too. These reflected badly on the paper, which prided itself on the accuracy of facts. All this was a world away from the principles (or their absence) of the tabloid press today. We never mentioned tangled domestic situations, that there might be estranged family relations, or than anybody deceased with an obituary in our paper was other than well-respected and liked.

Mr Godber also had a devious strategy: he knew that the way the obituary was set out and written, those who knew the deceased could decide if it was too short and missed out on some vital data. They then wrote to the Editor with more facts, which could be used to help fill the next issue. Long obituaries were not news for those who did not know the deceased, for they were not going to read that part of the paper anyway.

The Editor knew his readership well. Names of the living or dead, strangely enough, helped to sell more papers. Our circulation rose. More people, it seemed, would buy the local paper to read their names in print when they had attended a funeral and to make sure that their name was spelled correctly than would glance at a sensational front page scoop.

"Initials, don't forget the initials," rang out behind me from the chief reporter as I went to stand, cold and reverential at a church or chapel door, to collect the names of those attending, their relationship to the deceased, and which, if any, organisation, they were representing.

With small villages in the locality of the county town being full of intermarried inhabitants who had lived there for generations, the chances were that a very few surnames – and a good many first names too – would be shared by almost everybody. The initials were vital if the wrong man was not to be buried, let alone attend his own funeral as a mourner. Of course, all those in the village would know every detail of family ramifications and pounced on any mistakes.

Often I shared the church door shift with a reporter from the *Courier*. This of course was strictly forbidden but it meant that we could manage to buttonhole everyone and then share the information by means of 'third blacks': we would insert two sheets of carbon paper, and trade our extra copies. In those circumstances, the rules about never sharing stories went out the window.

Actually, we often pooled information. There was a happy camaraderie and not much rivalry at the low level of junior reporters. But higher up, the senior reporters who had ambitions of moving on to bigger papers frowned on cooperation or collusion.

OVER THE years I traipsed through the streets of Aylesbury and knew the names of every street and back alley. I found my way to villages, hamlets and isolated farms. There was nearly always a cup of tea on offer. Once I was asked if I would like some homemade beetroot wine. It sounded disgusting, but there seemed to be no tea available, and most of those in the front parlour were obviously already drinking a toast to their late father and grandfather, judging by the number of empty bottles.

"I'm that sorry," said the farmer's wife as she returned to the room with a large floral china cup and saucer in her hand, "but we're right out of glasses." She stared stonily at the females in the room, but no one rose to collect empties and take them to the kitchen for washing.

The cup she handed me contained a red liquid. I took a sip. It was smooth, tasted and looked much like claret – not that I was much of a connoisseur of wine, but it was warming me up in the same way as a cup of tea would have done. "It's grandfather's special vintage beetroot wine," she told me proudly.

With the information I needed in my notebook, I headed for the doorstep. I had left my bicycle in the porch of the farmhouse. Surprisingly – or perhaps not – I found it very difficult to get on and balance. Luckily there was no one to see my erratic and wobbly journey down the farm drive. By the time I reached the road, I must have sobered up enough to navigate the Queen's highways, and managed to reach the office safely.

There were times when I was asked if I would like to view the body. Most people held some sort of wake in the house, and the coffin was usually in the front room. Usually the tea and my interview took place in the warm kitchen at the rear.

Once I attended the funeral of a well-known gypsy grandmother. Her eldest daughter had left the roving life of caravans and lived in a modern prefab on a council estate. As I went down the suburban street, I could see lots of curious onlookers at their front doors or in the tiny front gardens behind the wire fences. All down the road were parked caravans, their horses enjoying the grass on the verges. There were also some smart and flashy cars – some held together with string and a prayer – lorries and even a grand Rolls-Royce of early vintage. A big crowd of men stood in the garden of the house I had to go to, and when I introduced myself, I was ushered into the tiny kitchen. Here was a cluster of loudly wailing and weeping gypsy women in a variety of colourful dresses and lots of dangling earrings and necklaces and masses of children milling round.

The male members of the immediate family were segregated from the females and were in the front room. That was where I went to get the details about the grandmother. No one was quite sure how old she was. Then I had to go to the front verge and write down the inscriptions from the dozens of enormous floral tributes. Many of these wreaths had the same names on them, but my guide explained that they were a very big family and most of the fathers and sons had the same names. It was also obvious that the florist had written many of the names and inscriptions as quite a few of the older men were illiterate, but more than sharp when it came to bargaining over horses or knowing how much change they were due in shops.

By the time I had finished, the black glass funeral hearse, drawn by black horses with nodding feather head plumes, had arrived and I hastily scribbled on while the coffin was loaded, the tributes were placed beside it and overflowing on to the top. As the men left the house and the garden, formed a procession behind the hearse and set off at a snail's pace, I must admit to thinking how those floral tributes had probably given several florists their profits for the week, and how their inscriptions were going to add quite a lot to my wage packet that week too.

THERE WAS another death which I can recall vividly, but for entirely different reasons.

One of our routine tasks was to go to the smaller villages on a weekly or fortnightly basis, and collect items of news from such sources as the vicar, the school and the local shops. The idea was that we maintained links and so should anything really exciting happen, our contact would let us know. I soon realised that to some of my contacts, I was just a weekly nuisance to be got rid of as soon as possible. So unless it was a vital contact like the vicar, I dropped these and tried to cultivate people who were pleased to see me, sometimes gave me a cup of tea and a cake while I waited for the return bus, or even those like the shop keepers or the postmistress who usually knew everyone in the village, who was related to whom, who didn't speak to whom due to ancient feuds, and whether there were likely to be any weddings or funerals in the offing.

My favourite fortnightly call was to an isolated village where there was a delightful elderly couple named Perkins whose home was adjacent to the bus stop. They always offered me a cup of tea and a chance to use their toilet while I waited for the bus back to the office.

Mr Perkins had been connected with many of the local organisations. He was a former clerk to the parish council and to the parochial church council but, now in his nineties, he spent most of the time sitting by the coal fire in the black-leaded grate and looking forward to my visit to bring him the news he was supposed to be supplying to me. No reporter had had the heart to take his name off the list of contacts for a good many years – and of course the cup of tea helped Mr and Mrs Perkins to remain popular with the press.

I used to hope that my other calls would not delay me because I found the couple's reminiscences of their young days delightful, especially of their years of courting. He always called her Mother, though they had no children, and they behaved with quiet courtesy to each other.

The kitchen cum living room was filled with objects from a long life in the same house. Pride of place over the mantelpiece was a blown-up photograph of the couple on their diamond wedding day, which had been taken by the *Herald's* photographer. A much smaller sepia one on the sideboard showed the happy young couple on their wedding day. The frame of the one over the fireplace was an unusually broad and highly polished wooden oval with a gap at the top like a horseshoe. One day while I sipped my tea and chatted, Ned – Mr Perkins – saw me looking at this. "The council carpenter was going to throw that out," he explained, gesturing towards the frame. "When we got the indoor lavvy, he was going to chop that up – after all my wife's years of polishing it."

So that explained how the good bit of mahogany which had graced the seat of the outside privy was turned into a distinctly different picture frame. The couple saw nothing incongruous in their judicious example of recycling.

One cold winter's day, I called as usual for my tea, and Mrs Perkins brought just two cups instead of the customary three on her tray. But I could see that Ned was having forty winks in his fireside chair and looked too comfortable to be roused for his tea. We chatted quietly so as not to disturb him and Mrs Perkins told me more about how they both grew up in the village and had been to school together.

When I heard the familiar deep diesel engine throb which told me that the bus was grinding slowly up the hill, I said good-bye to Mrs Perkins and rushed out of the house in case there was no one else at the stop and the bus sailed on past.

But as I went down the path, Mr Black Jr was coming up. His hearse was parked just beside the bus stop.

"Beat me to it for once then," he remarked jauntily as he

doffed his trilby and raised his hand to knock on the door of Ned's cottage.

Realisation struck me as I put out my hand to stop the bus. Ned wouldn't be waking again for his tea; he had died quietly in his sleep a short while before I arrived and, as ever, his polite wife had welcomed me to their house.

Because of the couple's diamond wedding report, I knew that Ned's obituary would be waiting for me in its slot in the morgue. It would be complete with the details of his long life and association with the village, so all I would have to do was put that day's date in the space left for it.

How peaceful he had looked and how serene Mrs Perkins had appeared. Now there would be one less call on my list of contacts – but I would miss him more than any of the others.

WEDDINGS, COURTS
AND COUNCILS

MARCH WAS wedding month – not for any romantic reasons, but because it was the end of the financial year. If you married before 31 March, both you and your groom or bride could claim full year tax-free allowances. But March was often Lent as well and many Church of England clergy, those well-known guardians of morality, stipulated there could be no organist, no choir, no bells and of course no floral decorations in the church in the weeks leading up to Easter, even for a wedding.

So in one corner you found the mother of the bride who would want the full traditional wedding for her daughter, while in the other was the daughter totting up the substantial amount of money the couple would get back from the Inland Revenue – as good as a dowry and very useful in the late post-war period. That left fathers of the bride trying to keep the peace between a tearful wife and an argumentative daughter, all the while thinking, no doubt, about the grand and expensive reception.

But money was a persuasive incentive and the number of

weddings quadrupled in March. Practically, for us, this meant many brides got only a brief mention in the *Herald* of the fact that their wedding even took place if it was in March, but during the rest of the year, we wrote up weddings with as much detail as we put into obituaries. We had a form which we handed out to brides, or more usually the bride's mother. If she filled it in correctly, it gave all the details we needed. Some brides' mothers were so caught up in the importance of the day that they would attach sheets of fragrant handwritten notes. We never used any of this but sometimes it was entertaining to read.

Writing up weddings was another of my weekly tasks. Like the obituaries, I soon learned to bash out wedding reports with the brides in white lace and the bridesmaids in matching pink dresses, and not forgetting to mention everyone's name and relationship and to get all the initials right. The challenge was to write a different intro for each report by picking out one of the facts on the form and leading the story with that. It made for some very convoluted sentences but was better than the boredom of Miss So-and-So in white, given away by her father with six bridesmaids, marrying Mr So-and-So who had his brother as his best man.

There were traps. One of my short-lived female predecessors had forgotten to look at the date of the wedding on the form, which the bride's mother had handed in far too early. The *Herald* had the couple married off weeks before the ceremony and had to print an apology as well as giving the wedding, when it happened, a much longer write-up than normal. In the dim past, there had also been a careless chap who had mysteriously managed to mix up the name of the best man and the bridegroom and hitched the bride to the wrong fellow. That was exceptional (and not at all certain that it hadn't been intentional) but it was all too easy to come unstuck among the relations, and muddle up sisters with sisters-in-law.

God could be puritanical about the wedding reports. If the bride and groom had the same address, we omitted this. Once, when the bride was a Miss but her son was to be a page boy, God struck out their relationship, and in another he removed the whereabouts of the reception as it happened to be at the home the bride and groom were sharing. How attitudes have changed.

Of course any error in a wedding report, in the eyes of the mother of the bride, was possibly the worst crime anyone could commit. One of my reports included a description of the bridesmaids' dresses (all eight made by the bride's mother), their bouquets and matching headdresses. I thought of the woman beavering away at her sewing machine for months before the great day, and probably enduring tantrums and tears with the innumerable fittings. Bridal shops were few and far between and helpful events like bridal fairs had not been invented. So the bride's mother also had to do the research on where the reception was to be held and how much everything was going to cost. It was still quite usual for the family to do their own catering with a friend making the wedding cake.

But for this particular wedding write-up, somehow between my typewriter, Bill's pencil, God's overview and the typesetting, a vital line was missed. The error wasn't even noticed when the reader and his boy read the galley proofs and when we checked the page proofs.

In the calm of a Friday morning, an incandescent bride's mother stormed the office and almost attacked God with a rolled copy of his own newspaper. We had told the world that the bride and the bridesmaids were identically dressed solely in white and red roses with trails of small-leafed ivy.

Mr Godber of course apologised profusely and promised to run another, accurate account of the wedding in the next week's paper together with a large photograph showing all the satin dresses and the bouquets of roses and ivy. "I assure you, madam," we heard him grovelling, "there is absolutely no reason to think that the bride and her attendants were other than properly dressed."

"I imagine it all depends on where the ivy trailed," Bill had said laconically when shown the report by a snorting God. "That would have been the picture," he told me as he reassured me that the error was not my fault. It should have been spotted so much earlier in one of the many foolproof checks. But he also quickly grabbed a few spare copies of the paper to clip the offending wedding report and send it immediately to suitable publications and so earn himself a guinea of two.

A COUPLE of years into my reporting career, when I had proven myself competent and reliable enough to report on the serious mistakes, malevolence and misdemeanours of our area, I started running into other journalists regularly. One of those I came across was Mr Frederick Throg, who was the proprietor of the *Gazette*, a small tabloid in a small town in the next county. He was a squat, older man with a round face and even rounder protuberant eyes, so it was no surprise that the younger journalists of the area nicknamed him the Frog. But in my mind he was always Mr Toad, for summer and winter, he wore a luridly patterned three-piece suit of heavy tweed. It contained orange threads, which matched his luxuriant bushy sideburns.

I first came across him – or rather he came across me – in the jury box of the County Court building. Every week it housed the Magistrates' Court, but this court was suspended when the Quarter Sessions and the County Assizes descended on Aylesbury with full judicial pomp and ceremony. Then the members of the press were relegated to a couple of backless benches behind the solicitors and a long way behind the barristers. But with the magistrates sitting, there were far fewer people in the Georgian courtroom and we were allowed to use the jury box. It had high wood-panelled sides and was like the old church pews with their small door entrances and private interiors. Long squab leather cushions padded the seat and the bench had a back, making it a far more comfortable area in which to spend a long day scribbling in a notebook.

Underneath the cushions were always a few piles of copy paper, which we secreted there so that during the absences of the magistrates we could start writing our stories in longhand and hope the printers could accept them. Theoretically during their absences the magistrates were discussing the case and possible sentence. But the recesses came regularly around eleven o'clock and again close to 3.30pm, and if the courtroom was quiet, we could hear the suspicious clink of cups. We dubbed these recesses 'pee and tea' breaks. Of course we dared not leave the courtroom in case the Bench returned in our absence, announced the verdict and sentence and the next case was called.

The day came when it was just Mr Throg and me in the somewhat private panelled confines of the jury box. He had the ability to jot down shorthand verbatim at a fast rate with one hand, while the other strayed round and about my person. Since I was similarly engaged with shorthand squiggles and trying to keep up with the statements, and using the other hand to steady the notebook on my lap, it was difficult to fend off his advances. Sexual harassment had not yet reached the statute books, so all I could do was make sure I never got trapped in the jury box with him again by either using some of my colleagues as a human shield between us or going to sit on the real press bench.

But Mr Throg got his comeuppance in a very satisfactory way some weeks later. This time it was the important Assizes in the same courtroom with the robed and bewigged judge on the throne-like seat in the middle of the dais for the judiciary, flanked by the Lord Lieutenant of Buckinghamshire in his dress uniform with sword, and the High Sheriff.

The members of the press were of course relegated to our hard bench, and I had put as much distance as possible between Mr Throg and myself. Sitting at the end also meant an easier writing position for we all squashed up together with elbows clashing. Mr Throg was somewhere in the middle, as usual already perspiring in his thick tweed outfit. The courtroom smelled of paint, for all the woodwork had been freshly varnished for the Assizes.

"All rise!" the court clerk called out as the judge was about to enter from a door behind the dais. There was a silence and a long pause as the police stood to attention smartly, the barristers adjusted their wigs and gowns and lolled against their leather seats with padded backs. The jury rose in an uncertain way – extras in the dramas about to unfold who didn't yet know their parts or what was to happen. We, who had been in the room so many times before, heaved ourselves up from the bench, clinging on to the sloping wooden shelf in front of us where the notebooks rested.

Something was digging hard into the back of my knees as I watched the ceremonial entry of the judge and attendant VIPs. The scenario reminded me of the *Wizard of Oz*. It was hard not to giggle as the Lord Lieutenant followed the red-robed judge into the silent court, for the Lord Lieutenant's full dress uniform was black with yards of silver braid and silver chains, and he wore a sword and spurs and clanked as he walked. Someone ought to have provided the Tin Man's oilcan. My imagination gave me a Cowardly Lion in the person of a red-faced farmer, nervous on his debut in such exalted company, and obviously terrified of making a mistake by doing the wrong thing against tradition. I did hope he could get his courage up as the Lion did. Lastly, in waddled a large woman in a big hat, skewered on with pins and covering a haystack of unruly hair. Her arms were working as hard as those of the Scarecrow, as she passed her portmanteau of a handbag from left to right while managing not to drop her gloves or the glasses she clasped.

The courtroom remained silent. No one could sit until the judge did. Suddenly there was a thunderous crash behind us. The press bench was up-ended on the floor. We all turned and started to pick it up. But there in the middle, where Mr Throg had been sitting, were firmly attached two ovals of hairy material. The tweed of his trousers had stuck so tightly to the bench that it had risen with us — that was what I had felt behind my knees. When the material could not longer take the strain, it had parted company with the rest of the trousers and stuck to the varnished and still slightly sticky bench.

Mr Toad, unaware of his part in the drama, bent over the bench, in the process mooning the judge. A gasp went round the room; he probably felt the draft. At any rate, he sat down in haste, the cheeks on his face as red as the posterior he had revealed to the company. He was unable to rise for the recess until a kindly policeman produced a large black macintosh. He scuttled sideways out of the court and back to his hometown and his newspaper with his embarrassment hidden under this garment. I never saw him in the court again. But there was more, much more to come from the Frog tabloid.

THE ASSIZES were always a time of ancient pomp and ceremony. The robed and bewigged judge, with a page boy to hold up the back of his robe to stop it from trailing in the street, processed with his entourage from the Judges' Lodgings, a tall house with imposing rooms set in a garden behind the civic buildings, accompanied by a gaggle of barristers, officials and local dignitaries. This was dressing up on a grand, adult scale. The Mayor donned his robes and chain for the occasion, and the Lady Mayoress had a new costume, chosen to accommodate her smaller chain, and a new hat. The aldermen also wore robes.

Leading the way was the Chief Constable followed by about twenty policemen, all managing to march smartly in step and carrying the traditional wooden staves topped with an iron pike and a black tassel. Traffic stopped as the procession made its way to the parish church of St Mary's for a special service in which prayers were said for the judiciary to be fair and just.

We watched the procession start, took a few short cuts to get to the church first and would have been sitting in our reserved pews waiting for them except that we had been told to wait at the church porch until the saintly procession was inside and its participants settled in their places. After the service, the policemen formed a guard of honour with their pikes for the judge and the rest of the procession to pass through before they made up the back of the parade. Then the poor chaps had to rush round getting back on the beat or off to their respective villages on pushbikes. It was probably a good time for burglars, with most of the police force occupied elsewhere for some hours.

One year there had been some alterations to the church and the iron cage in the corner of the porch where all the pikes were usually kept when the policemen entered the church was no longer there. Seeing there was nowhere to put their staves, a sergeant, seeing that the rest of the procession was hard on their heels and marking time on the church path unable to gain entrance while the police blocked the way, suggested they just pile them up in the corner.

That done, we took our places. The organ played and the clergy and choir had began their procession down the aisle when there was thunderous noise which went on and on. The pile of pikes had toppled; the porch looked like the old game of spillikins with six-foot poles tangled up. The woollen tassels had caught in the blades of the pikes, making it impossible to separate the sticks and pick them up. A number of policemen were despatched to sort out the muddle and through the hymns we could hear the clatter as pikes were pulled upright only to fall again. It made for an interesting service. The next time the Assizes rolled around, there was again a cage in the corner of the porch.

Sadly, any chance of a repeat performance of the tumbling pikes ended years ago when the pikes, and the tradition, were retired. Now there's only a solitary representative on display in the local museum.

THE CASES at Quarter Sessions and Assizes were always for serious offences; often we had heard the evidence in the Magistrates' Court before the case was committed to a higher court. We were well-schooled in what we could and could not print to avoid prejudicing a case and finding ourselves in the dock for contempt.

It was the job of one of the junior reporters to collect the list of cases for the weekly Magistrates Court on the evening before the court sat. It meant hanging about for ages in a bleak waiting room at the local solicitor's office because often the list was not ready. The head of the firm was the Clerk to the Court and very particular that the list could not be handed out until he had double-checked it.

The receptionist used to titillate us with remarks such as "There's something really interesting tomorrow." But I soon learned that her definition of interesting wasn't the type of crime that would set a tabloid journalist's antennae twitching, but more about poachers being caught potting at game the wrong time of year. The crime of killing conies – somehow they always sounded more exotic than mere rabbits – was a regular entry; the charge sheet usually ended with 'and taking game on a Sunday'.

Many of these ancient laws have long since been repealed, but even then they had an air of the sixteenth century and gentry keeping tight rein on their estates and tenantry. I almost expected the punishment still to be exile to Australia or worse.

In reality, the list was a long agenda of minor motoring infractions – speeding, illegal parking and other misdemeanours were still dealt with at the Court – although thank goodness most defendants wrote in pleading guilty and ready to pay the fine.

Something like minor shoplifting or disturbing the peace always resulted in a paragraph or two on the front page of the paper. The court's punishment might have been a small fine or being bound over to keep the peace, but the real punishment was when relatives and friends read the report of the case in the paper. The casual attitude to ASBOs or Community Service had not surfaced. A couple of times, I had white-faced and shaking defendants approach me after the court hearing with the plea, "You won't be putting my case in the paper, will you?" All I could do was tell them that the Editor was the one who decided what should be printed, but that it would be disastrous to approach him because then he would have to print their case or stand accused of being coerced. They had to sweat it out until publication day.

Over the years, reporters got to know the names of those who came to court regularly, and often for the same offence. At one of the small monthly magistrates' courts held in a specially built Victorian building behind the police station in quite a remote village, we met Salome – a very exotic name for a rather ordinary woman – who ran the brothel. Her sister, Delilah (their parents were obviously God-fearing folk, which was probably why the girls had gone to the devil), was also in the same line of business but there was great rivalry and jealousy between the two and their extended families.

I don't remember Delilah being charged with importuning but she always seemed to attract trouble. She was often in court for fighting in one of the rather seedy local beer houses. Not that she was any good at it, but as soon as she had taken a drink or two, she got argumentative and would resort to fists or bottle-throwing. She had been banned on many occasions, but she was a regular paying customer and landlords would extract a promise of good behaviour from her and she would be back in circulation again.

No solicitor had ever been found who could persuade her not to take to the witness stand. Delilah always wanted to put her side of the story at great length, with too much emphasis on the fact that none of it was her fault, a great many asides and irrelevant bits of evidence, so she was a very unreliable defendant. She always lost her case.

I think she had watched too many American films with dramatic court appearances and considered that the English stiff upper lip and insistence on no dramatics did not make the case interesting for the spectators or the Bench. She could address the magistrates with flashing eyes, tears if required, and certainly extremely generous décolletage for so early in the morning. She would lean out over the top of the witness box as if closer acquaintance with the Bench would help her case. Often it got her nothing more than a bored "Bound over to the Keep the Peace" from the chairman who had heard it all before. As he called out "Next" almost without drawing breath, a large police sergeant would bundle Delilah, usually still protesting her innocence rather loudly, out of the court room and away until her next appearance.

These long days in the small isolated courts were always a trial. The men used to dash down to one of the pubs in the village, but none of them were the sort where unattached females would find a welcome. Anyway I didn't like beer (shandy was all right) but the main trouble was than none of them offered a ladies' convenience.

The police sergeant who took Delilah from court saw me sitting on the wall in front of the building that housed the Magistrates' Court one lunch hour, and took pity on me. There was a large hallway at the entrance to the courtroom, and here the police had an office, an interview room, a holding cell and a lavatory. But since this facility was really for the use of prisoners being taken to the court, it had an outward opening door and no lock – plus in the centre of the door was a large circular hole so that a police officer could keep an eye on his miscreant and make sure he was not either trying to get out through the barred window, or endeavouring to hang himself with his belt or tie from the water pipe by the ceiling. But this sergeant was a very kind public servant and regularly thereafter, when I visited this particular court, he would place his burly self firmly in front of the door of the lavatory so that I could have a private visit.

This room was certainly worth a visit, for historical reasons. No expense had been spared when the building was opened in 1880, and no alterations had taken place since. The magnificent china throne with its mahogany seat had written on the inside of its pretty blue and white floral pan 'The New Niagara'. It was a very apt name. At the side was a matching china pull attached to a long, strong chain going up to the high ceiling and a large galvanised water tank which seemed to be perched on inadequate curly iron brackets. Pulling the chain released a torrent of water that cascaded from the tank into the pan with a tremendous whooshing noise. It was near deafening and left nobody in doubt that the lavatory had been occupied. After a short interval the sergeant would remove the black woollen porthole of his coat which I had as my viewpoint and I was free to walk out. The long arm of the law may be the better-known phrase, but I was always grateful for the 'broad back of the police'.

LOCAL GOVERNMENT had more tiers than a posh wedding cake. They all met and we reported on as many meetings as possible from the top level of the County Council through borough and rural district councils to the humble parish councils. We also covered annual meetings, branch meetings of local organisations and special interest groups, just because we had received an invitation. It was difficult to rationalise some of them because the specialised subjects debated in great depth and often with a passion missing at the 'more important' bodies were of little interest to the population in general. But people did like to read their names in the paper, especially if it could be attached to being chairman or president of something. Luckily the Women's Institutes, the Towns Women's Guild and myriad other organisations which flourished locally, like the Electrical Association for Women (don't ask; I can't remember), would send in their reports which we could rewrite in *Herald* style.

In a perverse way, it seemed the smaller the organisation the greater its sense of importance. One of the parish councils I attended monthly had been thrust into the public eye because it had succeeded in getting a bypass for one of its constituent villages. Those living near the busy narrow street wanted it, the shopkeepers were against because they feared losing trade and every one of its seven councillors seemed to have a lot to say one way or another.

The parish had no village hall so the council met in the one-room local infants' school. The chairman and clerk were able to sit behind the teacher's desk, but the councillors and the press and any members of the public present had to wedge themselves in the rows of desks built for children. It wasn't conducive to comfort and one winter's night there was a dramatic development. A councillor who opposed the bypass got very irate and argumentative and tried to stand up to make his point more forcefully. He was a large gentleman in a thick corduroy suit and as he struggled to his feet his face went strangely red, he grasped his throat and then fell clumsily across the desk.

Another councillor, who luckily was the local doctor, rushed to him and with assistance laid the inert body on the floor. The clerk ran to the local phone kiosk to call an ambulance, but I think we all knew that from the way the doctor put a clean handkerchief over the poor man's face that the ambulance would be taking him to the mortuary. We press huddled at the back of the hall and then muttered something to the chairman about getting out the way, the bus was coming, and filed out.

Since this councillor had been an important local, thankfully I did not have to write his obituary because it took a long time to get the image out of my mind. Pete tactfully sent Len to cover subsequent meetings of this particular council, sparing me the discomfort of going back. He did tell me however that they had moved to the vestry in the church. It was very cold in the winter with only a paraffin heater. The church pews weren't very comfortable, but at least they were adult size.

The more important borough and rural district councils of course had their own chambers or varying size and grandeur. The County Council had a magnificent half-hoop amphitheatre in the same building as the Assize Court and was the room used when there was a long court list and the main court was unable to hear all the cases.

The only trouble with going to the County Council was not

knowing who half the councillors were. I had to jot down short memory aids, like 'lady in big hat on back row', 'chap with booming voice' and other less-than-polite comments. Then, at the end of the meeting, the reporters would nobble the poor clerk or his assistant and try to put names to these faces. Of course, if they didn't represent our local area, we ignored them – whatever they had said.

There was another parish council meeting which I remember for entirely different reasons. It met in a village hall that had a stage at one end, so in fact it was quite comfortable with the councillors sitting round a wooden table on the stage with a few assorted chairs for reporters around. At one time, we had sat in the body of the hall but it was difficult to hear what people said. Also in the interests of economy the clerk had suggested that most of the lights could be turned out and we could manage with just a one-bar electric fire on the stage instead of heating the whole hall. Needless to report, the fire was close by the chairman and far from the press.

On the night of this particular meeting, I was excited because my latest boyfriend had offered to meet me afterwards at the pub, and since he had a car I would have a lift home instead of hanging about for the bus.

I'd never really taken much notice of this village, but when I got off the bus in the twilight I thought I had better locate the pub so I could make my way there quickly after the meeting ended. To my horror I discovered there were several on both sides of the main road, so I would have to be brave and go in and out until I found the right one. In between the hostelries were churches of several denominations: Baptists, Methodists, Salvation Army and the Congregational Church. I wondered how such a small village could support both the drinkers and the religious.

The village hall was very dark as I walked between the rows of chairs put out for a concert and got to the steps at the side of the stage. The open rafters were hung with large and tattered flags. These were wafting in the up-draft from the electric fire, giving the whole area a ghostly look. It was hard to see where the stairs were but suddenly there was the chairman with a hand out to help me up on the stage. I quickly sidestepped as he seemed to be getting a bit too familiar and not letting go of my hand. So I nipped smartly up to my usual back-row seat where I was joined by two other reporters. We waited, notebooks poised.

The chairman opened the meeting. Immediately one of the lady councillors butted in. "I'm so sorry but my hearing aid battery has nearly gone." Councillor Miss Knobbs was very deaf and had recently had the latest NHS hearing aid which had a large battery in a box which she slung on a cord round her neck to rest on her ample bosom. "I want to save it as much as possible," she explained, "so could you please nudge me when someone is about to say something important and I'll listen."

No one liked to point out that everything said was supposed to be important. The chairman nodded, but looked exasperated. I remembered that he was a local farmer with by far the biggest acreage. He had come from Holland after the war and seemed to be very wealthy. He was not popular with the locals for he had grubbed up most of the hedges between the small fields and made a big acreage for cereals in the days when all the farms were mixed dairy and arable.

Just as we were about to start the meeting, he held up a hand and said we should start with the national anthem. We shuffled to our feet and loosely to attention and he started out in a booming bass voice and we joined in rather tentatively without any musical accompaniment. No sooner had we sat down but we had to jump up again for the second and third verses. The Dutchman knew all the words; unfortunately we did not.

The clerk started reading the minutes and I saw that Miss Knobbs appeared to have dozed off. Then suddenly the lights and the fire went out and the room was very dark.

"Has anyone got a shilling for the meter?" the clerk called out.

Several men struck lighters and matches, money was found and moments later someone could be heard crashing around in the kitchen looking for the meter.

There was no emergency lighting in the hall but our eyes were becoming accustomed to the dark and the high windows were letting in some moonlight.

"It's dangerous up here on the stage," the chairman shouted. "Little lady, you might fall off."

Before I realised what was happening, he had swept me up in his arms and was striding down the steps to the main part of the hall just as the lights came on. I looked up and saw the double doors at the end open and the chap who was meeting me strode in. It was as if the knight in shining armour had arrived. I wriggled down and ran off to cast myself in his arms. The effect was rather spoilt when I had to go back and get my notebook.

The clerk saved everyone's blushes by suggesting that the meeting should be adjourned "in case the electricity fails again, and Miss Knobbs will be able to take a full part next time."

– 5 –

IN THE DOG HOUSE

AFTER THE FIRST year, when everything was new and different, I found the pattern of news and events repeating themselves and, by the third and subsequent years, I didn't need a calendar to differentiate the seasons of flower shows and fetes from Christmas and everything in between. Every season had its key fixtures; every local knew the dates of the September County Show or the spring Duck Races.

It was flattering, by the time of my second or third visit to an event, when the organisers greeted me effusively with "You're the young lady from the paper," but I always held my breath because in the next breath it could be "You missed out the names of the tea ladies last year," or "You didn't put in the winners of the children's races." But just occasionally it would be: "I'm glad you came again. Last year's report was better than when the chap came earlier."

The officials at all these local occasions seemed to keep their positions year on year. They knew me, but I had to try and remember them from among the many other people I met each week. I tried to be methodical and develop a card index memory. But with most villages having about five surnames between all their inhabitants, I clearly needed something more subtle. In one place, most of the locals seemed to be called Harris. There were the Harrises at the farm and their sons, all with large families, who lived locally and worked for father. His brother had a coal round and seemed to employ all the other relations. But every Harris was a great supporter of the village and the Parish Council, the Parochial Church Council, the Horticultural Society and the Darby and Joan Club. Their wives ran the Women's Institute, did the church flowers, the teas at the Old Folks' Club and won the prizes for sponge cakes at the Horticultural Show.

Initials, initials – the importance of initials was ever in the forefront of my mind. So I tried to remember that Mr B W Harris was the patriarch (easy – I just pigeonholed him as Mr Big Wig.) The son of the coal merchant also bred boxer dogs and we often carried short paragraphs about his success at various dog shows, though he never got as far as Crufts. His wife's name was in the paper most weeks and to this day I cannot remember her initials because of the terrible error I made to her face. In my mind she was Mrs Dogs Harris, to differentiate from Mrs Eggs Harris at the farm and Mrs Coal Harris who sent out the bills for her husband.

After I had been writing the women's column for a while, I started to get invitations to speak about my job at small women's groups – an obvious fill-in for groups who could not afford to pay a speaker. God was all in favour and said as long as I kept mentioning the *Herald* by name and how good it was, I could do these talks.

I felt honoured but also terrified. To me, my job was routine and it was going to be hard to make it sound interesting to an audience of rather bored middle-aged women waiting for their cup of tea and cake and a chance to gossip. Despite spending ages preparing, making copious notes, I was still very nervous at the first talk, but elated by the applause and the number of questions my listeners asked. The next one was easier, and so on. By the time an invitation arrived to do another to a larger group at the WI where the Harris clan held sway, I was full of confidence and had my notes from earlier talks.

I sat waiting after we sang *Jerusalem* to a very out-of-tune piano with the president trying to conduct but kept swiping her large straw hat with her hand. Then there was a great deal of incomprehensible and boring business to go through. I looked at the clock at the back of the hall and realised that my twenty-minute slot had already shrunk to ten minutes. The president had warned me that I must not overrun, otherwise the tea in the urn got stewed. At last the agenda finished and Madam President rose to introduce me.

I stood. Drew a deep breath to start my introduction and blithely began: "Members of the WI and Mrs Dogs, thank you for your invitation."

The gasp and titters alerted me to my mistake. Instead of correcting it immediately, I got flustered and apologised, saying: "Sorry I meant Mrs Eggs," before starting the talk. But my concentration had vanished and, glancing at Mrs Harris, I could see she was seething. That was the shortest talk of the lot. I sat down after about seven minutes. Thankfully there were no questions. Tea was served and I melted away.

The WI sisterhood has just as much influence in its own patch as the Mafia, and word spread rapidly about my *faux pas*. Whether the rank and file found it outrageously funny or simply outrageous, I never learned. The invitations to speak, however, dried up instantly.

ONE THURSDAY when I was proof-reading and skimming through the many small classified adverts, I saw 'Portable typewriter for sale, £2/10/- o.n.o.' My mind was not on the rest of the adverts. It was trying to decide whether, if I laid out two pounds and ten shillings of my own money, I could save myself a few hours writing out reports. There was an address but no phone number, so as soon as we finished work at noon on Friday (and had been paid) I caught a bus to the road where the typewriter's owner lived and hoped that it would not be a wasted journey.

I rang a bell and was pleased to hear someone coming to the front door. So many of my visits when writing obituaries had been in vain. A bit of a face appeared at a crack in the door and a surly voice said, "Yes?"

"About the typewriter," I said. "Is it still for sale?"

The door was flung open. A man with a sandwich in one hand stood there.

"Have you got cash?"

"Yes," I replied. I was a bit dubious. Was I being asked to pay before seeing and trying out the typewriter?

"Well there's a bloke says he's coming back soon when he's got the money, but you can come in and have a look."

We went into the dining room and there on the table was the typewriter with the lid of its case. I looked, fed in a sheet of paper and did the usual 'Quick brown fox' jumping over the something or other that used all the letters of the alphabet. Well, they all came out as they should and the keys didn't stick like those on the old machines at the office. Most satisfying, the 'O' did not leave holes in the paper. The office typewriters did, neatly removing the centre of every 'O', upper or lower case, and leaving a sprinkle of confetti on the table top. If the copy had lots of Os, it made quite a pretty pattern when held up to the light but it made something of an obstacle course for the subs' pencils.

As it was, this typewriter seemed all right to me. It had a ribbon with plenty of ink left so that the piece I had typed so quickly was very black and legible. I was anxious to complete the deal before the other buyer came back with the money.

The man said that he had thought of writing a novel, and that was why he got the typewriter. But recently he had purchased a motorbike and had to sell the typewriter to pay the installments on it. "I bought a spare ribbon so I'll throw that in – for free," he said emphatically.

Thinking about it afterwards, I realised that this salesmanship had won me over, but then again, what use would the new typewriter ribbon have been to him without a machine to use it in? I counted out the money, and he snapped the plywood cover in place over the frame and picked up the typewriter by a leather handle, indicating that I should lead the way back to the front door.

As soon as I was outside, he put the machine on the step and closed the door very quickly. I picked it up and went down the path towards the bus stop. He might have called it a portable, but in my eagerness I had not noticed that the machine was attached to a thick wooden base by very large metal bolts. Certainly it was portable – the strong leather handle was necessary – but it was more portable to someone used to training with heavy weights than someone like me walking on high heels and with a handbag in one hand.

Over the next few months, I felt my arms must have grown several inches as I heaved that typewriter on and off buses to various jobs and home in the evenings when I was behind and needed to clear my notebook. But it did add to my popularity at any job that involved lists; by using extra carbons, I could rattle off copies for my reporter friends. These extra 'blacks' earned me the odd cup of coffee in a café or even half a shandy occasionally.

It wasn't that my colleagues were tight, just that they were perennially broke. Whereas I, living at home, had fewer expenses than those in digs.

Clothes were a case in point. Women either washed clothes by hand, because no one had a washing machine, or if you were wealthier or lazier or both, you sent larger items to the laundry. Lads, on the other hand, were, well, lads.

Dave of trumpet fame had hardly any special clothes except a second-hand dinner suit which was essential for playing with the dance band. He had only one dress shirt and his landlady was supposed to do his laundry, but after she had put the stiff shirt through her mangle and then scorched it with her flat iron, he was in a quandary. If the shirt went to the laundry, there was the extra cost, he would be without it for a week and he might lose cash from missed band engagements. But he had no means of ironing it himself. He solved his problem with typical ingenuity: he would wash the shirt in the bathroom basin, hang it up to dry over the bath. Then he lifted the mattress from his bed, lovingly spread the shirt out as smoothly as he could, rolled back the mattress – and slept on it.

WITH THE regularity of something set in stone, I learned that each village had several occasions that a reporter would attend. The fête season followed the spring fairs, and then came the horticultural shows, jumble sales and more up-market Christmas bazaars and sales of work. At every one of these money-raising efforts, there would be the popular home-made cake stall – always the first to sell out – and, under different names in different places, the bric-a-brac or white elephant stall occasionally masquerading under the name of Antiques if the stallholder had managed to collect anything better than rubbish.

Not everyone shared such optimism on the quality or indeed saleability of goods offered for sale. It was like a bizarre serial to follow some of them around. What had not sold at one function would often be passed over to another in the same area.

I remember seeing a hideous vase with purple blotches given pride of place on one of the Objets d'Art stalls at a rather pretentious fête in the overgrown garden of a local manor. Apparently it had been donated by the lord or lady of the manor, who had also had a hand in pricing it. By the end of the afternoon, it was looking lonely in the centre of the depleted stall.

Some weeks later, the same vase caught my eye on the Antiques and Collectables table of another fête. Sadly but predictably, by the autumn 'bring and buy' for another local charity, it had dropped down to the white elephant, and there was a large chip on the rim.

I also watched the travels of a particularly nasty tin tray, rusty underneath, with puppies decorating it and unravelling wicker handles to carry it. Somehow at one of the shows I was inveigled into buying a raffle ticket; the first prize was something really good and there were to be 'numerous other prizes'. I had to stay on to get the winner of the first prize, which had been donated by a local firm anxious to get its name in the *Herald* without having to pay for it. I beetled over to the lucky prize winner together with Michael, who was to take his photo getting the prize from the sponsor, and was conscious of other raffle numbers being read out and people climbing on to the stage.

One number was read out several times, and I realised it was mine. "Hurrah!" I thought. I never won anything, so I made a hasty excuse to leave the group and go to the stage. Then I could see the prize being held up – it was that ghastly tray – so I passed the ticket on to a younger member of the first prize winner's family and asked them to collect it. As the poor child climbed on to the stage with my ticket in hand, the organiser boomed down the microphone, "You're only supposed to win one prize and your family scooped the best anyway. Let someone else have a chance." The child retreated. And all that for one measly tray that couldn't even be sold for a few pence.

THE HIGH spot in the summer of 1953 was Queen Elizabeth's Coronation. I had auditioned and got a part in a pageant that was to be the highlight of our local celebrations. I explained to God shortly after I started as a reporter that I was supposed to go to a number of evening rehearsals, and also would need time off to take part in the performances, so perhaps I should pull out? It had not occurred to me when I got the job that so much of my life was going to be dictated by evening and weekend jobs and I would always be juggling social life with work. But God liked his staff to be involved in local activities and so I was allowed to have a regular weekday evening off for rehearsals and the performances in the gardens of a local school.

Why, with so much evidence that it is not always hot and sunny in an English summer, should organisers decide that an outdoor pageant of The Queens of England would be the most patriotic way to mark the occasion, it is hard to conceive. Of course it rained, and rained, and the audience got wet and left in droves during every performance, so that by the end of each evening only the stalwart cast remained, getting more and more sodden and depressed.

But I did get my name in our rival, the *Courier*, as a Greek goddess, and a tiny mention that my voice was loud and clear, unlike some of the other members of the cast. Luckily our Greek robes were voluminous and didn't fall to pieces in the rain like some of the other costumes. Anything using crepe paper was a disaster and also stained the skin of the performer.

Our paper had a fairly glowing report of the pageant (well, God knew it wasn't going to be repeated and the large cast wouldn't be together again), so Pete's review could be impartial and quite kind. The story line was a bit convoluted: why Greek goddesses should be chosen to introduce the scenes of the various queens of England was not entirely clear, but that's what the author had thought up. The draped costumes and golden laurel wreaths weren't too bad in the drizzle; the courtiers of the different reigns had far more difficulty with sodden hose and doublets or crinolines made heavy with rain.

Goddess No 1: Jenny (left) with her fellow Greek goddesses in the Coronation pageant.

The pageant organisers had been in touch with the local hunt and nearly every scene included horses. Horses in the rain churned up the area of grass used as a stage so much that the performers had to pick their way through the ruts (and worse) to stage their scenes. But we all felt that we had added to the Coronation celebrations in a practical way, and it did get me out of reporting on the endless street parties and children's fancy dress competitions and sports with all the long lists of winners that these activities had to include.

Unfortunately someone with a long memory must have squirreled away the fact that a junior reporter had appeared as a goddess, and it came back to haunt me a couple of years later.

We all found it difficult to write criticisms of the various local dramatic and operatic offerings. Luckily with concerts we usually

115

only printed a copy of the programme and the names of those taking part and were not expected to become music critics overnight, nor to comment that the singers were apparently unaware of the conductor or that the string section had a far too democratic approach to tuning their instruments.

Early on, I had learned that amateurs, even when they say they welcome criticism of their performance, do not. They expect nothing but praise. Occasionally, when reading one of our reports about a school play, I wondered why the place was not a drama college turning out first-rate actors and actresses.

When it was my turn to try and tread softly on the merits or otherwise of one of these affairs, I thought I had the perfect solution. The performance of the lead actor in a local play was appalling, but conveniently he was also the play's author and producer. If I left out any mention of his acting but included his name in connection with the other two roles, what harm would there be in that? Plenty, as it turned out, and it led to a showdown in God's office.

The actor's name was Nigel Clavering. I knew him vaguely because he had also appeared in the Coronation pageant, as a courtier in a scene where Queen Anne heard the news of the victory at Blenheim.

On the Friday morning when I was skimming through the paper and we reporters were having a good gossip, there was a summons for me to go to the Editor's office and to take my notebook. I tentatively knocked on God's door and immediately heard: "Enter." Nigel was sitting at the desk facing the Editor with a copy of our paper open at the relevant page in front of him. Before I could say hello, God announced me. "This is Miss Hogarth," he thundered. Nigel rose languidly and held out a limp hand for me to shake. I was still reeling from the fact that God had not only remembered my name, but had introduced me in such a formal way.

Nigel quickly brought me to my senses. "It is so unnecessary to write this sort of thing," he complained in a petulant voice.

Before I could utter a word, God interrupted. "I pass all the copy my reporters write and could see nothing libellous or untrue in the item about your play. I gather from my chief sub-editor that he too saw nothing wrong in the report, and in fact had spoken to our very talented young reporter as she had explained that few of the cast knew their words."

I was astounded. God was on my side, prayers had been answered and more. It had never occurred to me that the Editor considered I had any future in journalism. Had it not been for Bill's mature advice I might have been far more scathing of the production and written how bad it was and that the lead was the worst actor of all.

However, none of this was necessary. Nigel was a better actor off stage than on. He gripped his knees uneasily and looked at me with his big brown eyes like a spaniel who needed constant patting on the head. "I was very upset not to be mentioned in my own play, which I wrote and produced," he said *sotto voce*.

It was obvious he had quite an opinion of himself that didn't marry up with reality. The audience had been composed almost entirely of his relatives and friends. Of course they applauded, but it didn't mean that the play should be automatically exempt from any kind of criticism just because it was his creation.

A few more words were exchanged. I don't recall what was said. I do remember leaving God's office walking on air.

A few years later, I was to discover that Nigel not only wrote make-believe for the stage, he lived in a little time-warp all his own.

But it was his amateur company who had their revenge on me – they made me take part in one of their less awful productions. It was a masterstroke on their part, a triumph of sorts as I would not be able to write criticism of the production, and might get criticised myself.

It happened at least a couple of years later, when the Coronation and its pageant had long disappeared from everyone's memory. The company had decided to produce the well-tried Agatha Christie mystery thriller, *The Hollow*. Nigel was acting but not producing; that job had gone to another member of the company. He had been relegated to a small part in a large cast. Unfortunately the young woman cast to play opposite him got measles just before the final dress rehearsal, and it was Nigel who remembered that I had acted in the pageant.

Apparently he had telephoned direct to God who had realised that helping resolve an emergency for the cast could earn him –

and the *Herald* – some brownie points. That Nigel was connected with many local dignitaries and his father was a lord of the realm had some bearing on God's command that I take part.

That evening, I was excused diary jobs for the next week and was directed to go to the house of the play's producer. Maeve was a small, dark Irishwoman, a complete contrast to Nigel with his artistic temperament. She led me into the dining room where Nigel and a couple of other cast members were already sitting and drinking coffee. We exchanged slightly awkward greetings.

Maeve clapped her hands. "Work to do," she said and handed me a marked copy of my part. Her enthusiasm and vitality were infectious. We read through the couple of scenes in which Nigel and I would appear, and already I could see that this play was going to be so much better than any in the past, so perhaps it wouldn't be so bad appearing in it and also having to act with Nigel.

The play was staged, both the *Herald* and the *Courier* reviewed it somewhat sympathetically, and I was able to retire from the stage. As for Nigel, there was more drama ahead with him, but on this occasion he was the perfect gentleman.

WITH OUR weekly calls to the local villages in our neighbourhood in search of news, I must have met hundreds of people. Trying to remember their names and their particular reason for being included in the list of contacts was a headache.

Clergymen of all denominations were an obvious call in every village. In those days they were all Christian of one kind of other.

The smaller the church, it seemed to me, the greater their sense of self-importance. I soon learned about all the small non-conformist churches in the area, and however small their congregations, they were keen to have reports of their services, fund-raising activities or social events reported in our paper.

One Church of England vicar was helpful and also had a wonderful store of racy stories about famous people he had met, which he entertained me with while his stern housekeeper served us bitter and horrible coffee. But I did enjoy my visits and only wished I had been brave enough to take notes of what he told me since I have now forgotten. He lived alone in an enormous Gothic Victorian vicarage. It was before the Church of England had started selling off these expensive properties and housing the clergy in manageable property.

On my first visit, I walked up the long, once-gravelled drive under overgrown shrubs to reach the mansion. The front door had glazed panels of ornamental glass and the knocker was so large and high that I realised I would not be able to reach it. However, I spotted a handle at the side of the door and pulled hard. Inside the house and from far away I could hear the bell clanging mournfully. Then I waited and nothing happened, so I tugged again and decided that after the third time I would give up and explain to Pete that the vicar was not at home. But there was the sound of dragging footsteps and a face appeared moon-like on the opposite of the door but distorted as if in the Hall of Mirrors by the patterns and colours of the dirty glass. Then, with a screech, a bolt was drawn, a key turned slowly in a lock and the door opened slowly to reveal the housekeeper.

"I'm from the *Herald*, making a call on the Reverend Besum," I explained to the blank face in front of me.

"Next time call at the back," she said sourly and motioned me inside a cavernous, dark and damp smelling hall. She escorted me silently along dank passages cluttered with sacks of potatoes, firewood, dog baskets and past many closed doors. She stopped and knocked on the last one. There was no call to enter, but she opened the door to the vicar's study and shouted out: "It's a new young lady from the *Herald*," and left what appeared to be an empty room.

It was as vast as I imagined all the rooms must be. A small fire put up a spirited but ultimately doomed fight in the enormous grate. I could see my breath as I exhaled. Bookcases lined the walls and there were lots of chairs scattered around as well as a big table. This was covered with a chenille cloth that hung to the ground. The paraphernalia of sermon writing was strewn over the top.

One side of the cloth lifted up, and out peered a face with a clerical collar below. The Reverend Edwin Besum scrambled out from beneath the table, stood up and shook my hand. "I do apologise but sometimes it is necessary to be 'out' when I am in fact 'in'. Now what can I do for you?"

It was the first of many calls and although there was never any exciting news, just the regular services, or the proposed fête and Christmas sale, those visits were always a highlight in the routine.

"What do you think of my name?" he asked me once.

Before I could think of a suitable reply, he snorted and commented, "Just a cross between bosom and besom, but neither one nor the other. Like me," and again there was a roar of laughter.

He explained why he preached his sermon with his eyes shut. "The women's hats: where do they get such amusing headwear? And I like to follow the seasons as the artificial flowers come out for summer to the bits of fur in winter."

It was difficult to keep him to the point and he tended to forget important items of news such as the visit of the bishop. He had been a curate in the West End of London during the 1930s and had wonderful tales of the aristocracy and their antics – although I did wonder if he should not be repeating some of the stories since they probably were told to him under the seal of confession as he had served in a very High Church. He never let that get in the way.

OVER THE years, my basic Church of England upbringing was tested by the various Christian denominations in the area and the services or events I reported about. It was a reflex action when the strict Methodist minister said, "Let us pray," and I was immediately kneeling. There was none of the usual sound of the congregation creakily relying on their knees, as they slid from the pews to the floor, and I realised with a blush that everyone was waiting for me to get up and just sit with bowed head.

Whereas in the High Churches – what Pete scathingly

referred to as "bells and smells and covert Pope people", i.e. not Roman Catholics – it could be difficult to follow what the congregation was supposed to do. We joined in some processions round the church, but not others.

Singing of hymns was also fraught with problems. The title would be announced and everyone would rifle through books and I would think, "I know that one," when a completely different tune would start on the organ, piano or harmonium, whichever instrument they had.

The Jehovah's Witnesses prayed for the 'stranger in their midst' for a very long time, and I had no opportunity to answer back. The occasion was when a very young and scared-looking girl was about to go to South America as a missionary. I tried to talk to her at the tea and biscuits bit, but there were two minders who just kept saying she was going to convert the heathen and she looked at her feet, appearing to me for all the world as if she wished she hadn't been 'chosen'.

The Salvation Army Citadel services were much more jolly with the rousing hymns and the brass band.

FAMILIARITY IS one thing, but as my job became routine and there were fewer 'firsts', I missed the accompanying sense of excitement before a new task. It became harder to bring enthusiasm to the latest batch of weddings that had to be written up, or even to avoid becoming blasé in the face of the sameness of the cases at the local Magistrates' Courts. It was exciting the first time I had to sign the Official Secrets Act so that I could attend an electoral count, but then that too became mundane.

I got used to listening to people rambling on the telephone and trying to keep them to the point so that I could extract the basic news from their opinions.

Len got a prospective local borough councillor on the phone one morning. The man was explaining his reasons for standing and his philosophy on so many subjects and Len knew that whatever he said would be cut down to the standard number of words for each candidate. The rest of us were making 'wind up' signs with our hands as we all wanted to use the phone for important and urgent calls. At last Len was able to cut the caller short and, when the receiver was down, cut the candidate down in a few pithy sentences as a "stupid, long-winded nutter".

We were all busy typing or telephoning when he shouted out, "Are there one or two Ls in philosophy?"

He got a variety of answers, and I handed over the big, dog-eared Oxford dictionary which was always on the table. Len was silent for ages and I could see him leafing through page after page. "I've gone right through all the flipping Fs, and it's not there!"

Oh, the joys of a spell-checker on a computer. Even professional wordsmiths hit a blank sometimes; the secret was not to let on. Otherwise your colleagues were unlikely ever to let you forget, as Len discovered.

– 6 –

PICTURE THAT!

PICTURES IN THE papers – how they've changed in the last sixty years. Now we get them full colour, very large, digitally enhanced, transmitted by satellite or over the Internet and available instantly. Everyone has a camera with auto focus, auto zoom, auto flash, auto everything and halfway to having a mind of its own. You can take photographs and videos on your phone, for heaven's sake, and see and hear the results immediately.

What a far cry from my early newspaper days when standard newspaper issue were huge, single-shot plate cameras. The camera that the Herald provided for our photographer was as different to today's cameras as a mobile phone is from an ancient candlestick telephone. He always had his own Rolleiflex slung round his neck, but he had an ongoing battle over who should pay for his film. The impasse in the accounts department was one particular clerk who couldn't understand why so many rolls of film had to be used, especially when many contained only a few pictures with the rest of the roll thrown away after the film had been developed

125

by the photographer. "We need those pictures this week, not next, and I have to develop and print them up as fast as possible," Michael the photographer would explain wearily.

The old plate camera was difficult to carry, complicated to set up, and limited to shooting one picture at a time. But it did give a very sharp focus, which meant that when the photograph was reproduced in the paper, it was possible to recognise all the people it in. We could display these photographs – especially if it was a wedding group – in the window of the printing office; family and friends usually ordered a good many copies, all useful income for the company.

Pictures are strong selling points, so at an editorial conference, wreathed in tobacco smoke, the editor, sub-editor and chief reporter would assess the pictures. With luck, one would jump out as definitely front page material – a striking image that would grab a potential customer's attention and induce him to buy the paper. Next they appraised the wedding pictures; they would always be used because not just the immediate family but guests at the wedding would buy that week's issue as a souvenir of the event. In those days, few people took their own cameras to weddings, so the bride and groom relied on commercial photographers for their pictures. Actually Michael had quite a good and profitable sideline in wedding photography.

Printing photos on the old letterpress was a chore. The photo had to be converted through a process of acid etching into a metal negative image called a block. So the editorial conference had to take into consideration how many blocks would be needed, together with the number of hours available to the block maker to make them. He worked in an unheated wooden shed outside the machine room; accommodation which, like that of the photographer, had been added on to the original Victorian building. It must be said that neither of them was hugely impressed with that fact.

Michael finally managed to ditch the old plate camera with a little complicity from myself.

At my interview, God had told me that because men and women were on equal pay, there could be no discrimination about which jobs we attended. Somehow he conveniently forgot that it was always the girls who had to write up the weddings and the Women's Institute meetings, but that's by the by.

So not long after I started work and had started to attend and write up small stories, the chief reporter put my name down in the Bible beside an amateur boxing match. "I don't know anything about boxing," I complained to him. "Can't I do something else?"

"No," he said. "We're all busy that night. There's no one else."

Later I learnt that they were 'busy' at the pub where the landlord was putting on a special evening with (mildly) blue movies. It was invitation only, obviously, and the guest list included the officers of the local constabulary so that they wouldn't raid the pub that evening. These films would now be considered suitable viewing for any age, but the Lord Chancellor still censored all films and theatrical performances and there were many taboos about what could be seen by the general public.

So I set off with Michael to the function room attached to a big Victorian pub in a local village. We arrived in style in the *Herald* van as it was not a delivery evening. The luxury of not having to wait for a bus almost made up for having to go to a boxing match; almost, but not quite.

We were ushered in by a rotund gentleman with a cigar clamped between his jaws. I looked around in dismay. There were only two rows of chairs round the elevated boxing ring and behind them stood spectators drinking from pint glasses and smoking cigarettes and pipes. The front row seemed to be occupied exclusively by portly gentlemen puffing on cigars.

We had front row seats. The chairs were wooden and my full skirts with the layers of stiff petticoats stuck out all round me. It took ages to wash these petticoats in a sugar solution in the bath. Then when they dried it was an even longer task to iron all the layers of frills. The effect was pretty enough, but I felt overdressed, despite a number of coloured waistcoats and bow ties among those seated at the front, and out of place. I put my notebook and pencil on my lap and waited for something to happen.

Someone gave me a programme, and I asked this man if he would help me with the reporting. He asked me where the reporter was and noticed my confusion as I had to confess it was me. So he looked me up and down and commented something about "a dirty trick to play on a young girl." But he kindly 'marked the card' much like the tipsters did at the races because he was pretty certain who was going to win each bout. He was starting to give me a fatherly explanation about the weights and what would happen when there was a roar from the crowd and the first two fighters entered, wearing dressing gowns, and clambered into the ring. When they started hitting each other, I closed my eyes. It was horrible to watch, and I really didn't want to know what was happening. The crowd was roaring the fighters on and someone was hanging on to the back of my chair and banging it with excitement.

Michael put his big camera on the edge of the ring and focussed ready to get a shot, preferably of a knock-out. The noise was deafening and suddenly got louder. I looked up, and there almost on top of me was one of the boxers hanging over the rope with his nose gushing blood. It ran all over the lens of the camera and spurted in the direction of my notebook page dangling white and unused on my lap.

I think I screamed, got up and tried to get away. In the meanwhile, an official had come with a bucket of sawdust and was throwing handfuls about to soak up the blood.

By this point, the referee was holding up the other boxer's arm, and I gathered that the fight was over. The man who was going to help me with the report kindly gave me his telephone number, and I arranged to ring him in the morning and get the rest of the results, as well as the amount of money that was had raised for charity. I waited for Michael outside.

The next morning, after I had got the results, Met the Bus, visited the undertakers and also drunk my tea to give me courage, Michael and I went together to God's office. I showed him my blood splattered notebook and explained why I had left the job early. Michael put his exhibit – the old-fashioned camera – on the desk and invited God to look through the viewer. The lens, despite thorough cleaning, could not be properly restored and so the camera was abandoned, and from that day on he was allowed to take all the photographs on his own camera.

LOCAL HISTORY was another of those topics we could prepare in advance because it was hardly going to go out of date. One of our local butchers was the unlikely source of a regular column about Aylesbury's history called, with great imagination, The History of Our Town. We ran these whenever there wasn't enough news to fill the early pages. Mr Clump the butcher never asked to be paid; it was enough to have an outlet for his memories.

But Mr Clump was a busy man, so every so often a junior – usually me – was despatched to collect a few more episodes to have in hand.

The job went something like this. I would walk down the High Street to the butchers, hoping he would have no customers when I arrived because that would turn the assignment into a quick doddle. Somehow it seldom turned out that way.

Mr Clump's was a very old fashioned butcher's shop even then, with sawdust on the floor, carcasses hanging from a steel rail behind the well-scored wooden block and a slight warm smell of blood and off meat. Refrigeration was not in evidence. Incarcerated in a small wooden kiosk in one corner of the shop was Mrs Clump. More of her in a moment.

"Hello Mr Clump," I opened. "Have you got a few moments for another installment please?"

"Yes, been awaiting of you, my girl." His bucolic Buckinghamshire dialect was a joy to listen to, although some of the words needed translating. "Thought it was time I was atelling of the Christmas Fat Stock shows in the Market Square. All the animals had to come on the hoof, no moty transport then. Hens could go in carts and single pigs, but even the geese walked.

"Hello Mrs Smith," he said as a customer walked in, "a pound of your usual and how is Mr Smith these days?"

Just as I had got into automatic shorthand note-taking mode, with the pad resting on the edge of the butcher's block, I had to move it and remove the last couple of sentences. But it was vital to stay alert.

"Of course the cows and especially the bulls were the real reason for the show. Did you want some mince too, and I've got a nice bit of calves' liver. Of course the liver from the cattle then was real ox liver and tough but good for stews.

"Now I was just atelling this young lady, she's from the paper you know, about the Fat Stock show. We always competed to buy one of the prize-winning animals so that we could have the rosettes in the winder, and our customers knew where to come for the best meat for Christmas. That'll be three and thruppence, Muriel."

Muriel being Mrs Clump who also had to sift through her husband's conversation in order to write out a ticket for the meat and to take the money. Many customers were 'Account clients'; Mrs Clump had to know without asking whether to wait for the money to be handed over through a small slit in the glass front of her cage, or whether she was expected to find the right page in the invoice book and enter the details of the transaction for invoicing later on their notepaper headed 'Clump and Son – purveyors of excellent butchery to the gentry'.

The Mr Clump I spoke to was in fact the grandson of the founder and getting on in years himself; probably it had been his father who had ordered far too much headed stationery from our printing works and was loath to throw it away for a more modern approach. My mother had been an account holder for years – not that we ever thought of ourselves as gentry – and bills for meat would arrive erratically months in arrears. Sometimes the boy delivering the meat would also hand over a bill, but usually they came by post and father would open it.

"How much?" he would shout, aghast.

"Well, it must be the off-ration specials as well as all the meat I bought on the coupons," mother would explain. During and after the war, our household would sometimes be enormous, with relatives doubling up with the evacuees and billets, or it might shrink to less than the original family as live-in servants vanished and children went off to war or boarding school. Since it was impossible to check the butcher's bill, father said mother was to stop being an account customer.

What a loss of face! Mr Clump's only remark as she handed the cash to Mrs Clump was that we would no longer be eligible for the free calendar he gave to all his account customers. With his long memory, even as he was telling me more about the excitements of the Fat Stock show and the Christmas Poultry auctions, he managed to slip in that we must still be missing the calendar.

When we were running the extra Christmas pages, Mr Clump of course was a prominent advertiser, and it was easy to find plenty to write about his shop. However, he also had the most unusual window display a few days before Christmas, and before his customers collected their turkeys, geese, joints of beef and game.

Before the turkeys were plucked (though I suppose they must have been drawn or the smell in the shop would have been even more pronounced), they would be dressed in small woollen pullovers knitted by Mrs Clump and perched on butcher's wooden skewers so they looked as if they were running. On their backs would be placed small dolls, dressed in jockey's silks (sewn by Mrs Clump) holding strings of chipolatas which made the reins for the turkey's race. It was an amusing display; hygiene did not seem to be a problem. Usually our photographer or Mr Haddock would capture the picture, which could then be used in the last of our Christmas advertisement features.

The racing turkeys were a big hit with the children of the area who would come to peer in the window, while their parents, one hoped, would be attracted by the other window's display of the enormous carcass of the winning animal from the Far Stock show with its rosettes and certificates prominently displayed.

WE DIPPED into our own archives for another series that we used when there wasn't enough news for the early pages, which had to be printed on Tuesdays. We had '50 years ago this week', as well as '25 years ago this week', and even '10 years ago this week' if news was very thin. These features fell on my shoulders, to be written when I had an odd few minutes to spare.

My sources were the old bound copies of the newspaper which were arranged on big shelves behind God's desk. These weighty tomes did add gravitas to a dingy room and made the Editor at his leather-topped table look slightly more important. They were an almost-complete record. In the 1880s, there had been a fire at the original offices and printing works. This had left some gaps in the records, so the original '75 years ago this week' had had to be adapted to the volumes of the *Herald* that were available for reference.

Mr Godber always made a fuss about getting the relevant volumes down – but on no account were we allowed to haul them upstairs to the reporters' room where it would have been so much easier and quicker to consult them. As he rightly pointed out, they were historical documents. "Very valuable," he would stress.

So I had to work on the wobbly table that we used when we put the inserts in at Christmas time, but which by then was covered with vital bits of paper that Mr Godber had not got round to sorting or filing. Pushing these aside, I would open up the relevant volume where I had left off my research some weeks earlier. Even in this short while, more dust seemed to have collected on the book and clouds would rise as I turned the heavy and densely printed broadsheet pages.

Sometimes there seemed to be little of interest; other times I got carried away by a very long court report and forgot the time and the fact that I was only supposed to be getting short paragraphs for the feature.

What struck me was that occasionally there seemed to be a dearth of news for the weekly paper all those years ago. It did carry items of national news which presumably would be unknown to those who did not subscribe to a national newspaper such as *The Times*. But it also had long and dull descriptions of meetings, church services (including the sermon) and even longer lists of names of those attending funerals than we did. But sometimes there were amusing nuggets too. Often when I found the volumes for twenty-five and ten years ago, it almost seemed like the next episode in the serial as the same problems were making the news.

Because the bound copies stayed downstairs, I had to take a shorthand note and then transcribe it when I typed it out. But usually there was a gap between my getting the items downstairs and finding time to write them up. A pile of work – re-writes, weddings, etc – had a habit of appearing on my part of the table as soon as I left the room.

One Friday morning, I was reading the paper while waiting for the pay to arrive when I saw the heading 'Traffic Chaos at Cannon Corner'. Cannon Corner was the aptly named crossroads in the centre of Buckingham which anything larger than a horse and cart had a job negotiating; most lorries had to mount the pavement, while articulated lorries needed a couple of shunts. The locals avoided this road if possible and even the buses had been re-routed. The council was always discussing ways to make it wider, safer or part of a one-way system, but the matter was always deferred, either from lack of money, or because no one could think of a reasonable solution.

The news item spoke of a barrel of a cannon being purchased and then up-ended and embedded on the pavement at the corner. "This will prevent vehicles travelling too fast, and inconveniencing pedestrians as well as giving warning of the dangerous road conditions."

Funny – those words rang a bell in the back of my mind. So I turned to the early pages – and there was the very same paragraph in the '50 years ago this week' feature.

Panic. I started going through my notebook and found the relevant page. Somehow I must have forgotten to put the proper catchline on my copy.

I went to the lavatory for a think, and like a coward decided to say nothing until someone noticed. Surely one of our eagle-eyed readers would notice.

The following week was terrifying as I waited to be summoned by God for a dressing-down about my appalling careless error.

But nothing happened.

Except in the next week's paper, there was a paragraph from the council meeting stating that the situation at Cannon Corner had been discussed and been deferred to a future date when a decision would be made. Fifty years of prevarication continued.

BYLINES AND BLOOMERS

AS BILL, OUR sub, was always emphasising, the Editorial department was built on teamwork and loyalty to the *Herald*. I couldn't help noticing that as 'captain of the small team', he and his pal, Pete the chief reporter, somehow missed out on Sunday shifts or the really awful jobs that no one would volunteer for. They put our names down in the Bible and no excuse was ever good enough to get them to swop jobs with us.

We all had to write 'in the style of the paper' which really boiled down to memorising the order of priority in lists of names, the way of addressing various members of the clergy and councillors and how many spaces to insert after a full stop. When it was lists of helpers at the flower show or the Christmas bazaar, you knew that anyone with a title would have to come first. This became rather incongruous when I discovered, as I rewrote a report of the Women's Institute Group Meeting, that the woman in charge of the lavatories was the Honourable Miss Josephine Rigby. Naturally she had to head the list; others who had far more important duties and exacting positions just had to follow on. Lists of ladies started with the 'Mesdames' – even then an archaic description – followed by the Misses. There was never a Ms anywhere in those days: the term hadn't been invented.

No individual styles of writing were allowed in the belief that no one reading the paper should be able to tell which reporter had written which report. If any adjectives appeared, Bill's blue pencil would score them through heavily, and before he sent the report to the typesetters, he would call the culprit to his desk and deliver a public scolding.

It was a quick and humiliating way to learn what to write, to keep every sentence short and to the point, and never ever to write something that had not been checked for accuracy. But speed was very important too, so there was always a balancing act between getting the facts correct and getting the report filed. This became less of a problem as time went on, the repetition involved in writing very similar reports soon making their production a routine business.

The only time we could express ourselves was if we got assigned to write a 'crit' – criticism for something like a play or a concert, an art exhibition or a book review. Where the national dailies had specialists for this sort of thing, in the provinces we were all expected to chip in.

My knowledge of the arts was superficial but that didn't stop me from voicing an opinion as I sought to write authoritatively sounding criticisms of the local dramatic society's latest production, or the amateur orchestra's highbrow concert, an exhibition of blobs claiming to be modern sculpture or a book which I had had to skip through because it was so dull and boring or was far too complicated for me to understand.

With one dramatic society in particular we had to be very careful not to offend the producer or the players. Some years earlier, one of our reporters had been careless enough to state that the production would have been much improved if the actors had known their lines and that the prompt was the busiest member of the ensemble. The producer, who was vaguely related to the owner of the paper, stormed into God's office on the day of publication and threatened to withdraw the advertising for his drapery store, and also to bar any reporters from future shows, unless an apology or retraction was printed.

One of my earliest attempts to get around the problem of how to describe a very dreary farce without actually saying so was to write instead about the convoluted and far-fetched plot, which I hadn't actually followed properly, and then list the cast and the parts they played. Finally I padded it out with every name I could find on the programme from the scenery painter to the lady selling tickets at the door.

Bill had looked at my effort and then, instead of his usual abrasive lecture, had sat me down by his desk and rewritten the report. "I know what a tightrope we have to walk," he said. "It's the most difficult task in the book. It's no good really criticising them because they're amateurs and think they're doing their best.

"But remember they're taking money from members of the public and so ought to give a reasonable performance. You don't have to judge them as professionals but they ought to know their lines and direction and keep the production going without lots of hitches."

Then he gave me a few tips. Always sound as if you know the production and are comparing it with others that were similar; don't over-explain – write like you expect your readers to have a little knowledge themselves; throw in a few authoritative statements which you can usually get by reading reviews in the London dailies or magazines, and just adjust them to fit the circumstances. That advice has stood me in good stead ever since.

The thing about these crits was they were bylined. It was the only time our names appeared in print, and so it was always nerve-wracking the week after publication in case anyone was going to write in or visit the office and complain – as indeed Nigel did when he felt I had slighted him in my review. Nobody ever paid us compliments, which I suppose was a compliment in itself – as a hack you soon learn that 'no news is good news'.

THE FIRST two years I was with the *Herald*, it changed enormously. Both the classified and display advertising were growing and wartime paper rationing had ended, so the issues could expand to accommodate this growth. Yet another piece of machinery was bolted on to the original press, and seemingly attached to the ceiling, so the old flatbed could now print eight pages early on a Tuesday. Most of them would be the lucrative advertising, but there had to be enough editorial matter to meet our legal obligations. This continued to be a problem.

One Friday morning, we were summoned to God's office. We knew it was an important occasion because the owner of the paper and some of the people from the printing office were sitting squashed behind his desk. The editorial team stood awkwardly in front of it.

The proprietor softened us up by thanking us for all the hard work with the Christmas inserts and our efforts in helping the circulation to grow. "But we need to move forward to modern times," he boomed pompously, giving way to God to handle the official business of the meeting.

"We are going to have a features page," he announced with great aplomb, "and this is how it will work."

"By Monday evening, the features will be written and ready for printing on Tuesday morning. So I shall be extending my leader column on this page which means that I shall have to get the editorial written over Saturday morning or at home during the weekend to be ready. As you know, there is so much I need to do on Mondays with the post and sorting out you lot." Trust God to get in first and explain how much extra work it would mean for him.

"Pete," he pointed to the chief reporter, "I want a weekly topical newsy column of your thoughts and ideas." Pete blanched a little and wondered aloud what on earth that meant.

"Think up a good catchy title," said God, "and of course you will get your name under it." At this hint of fame, Pete stopped looking so worried.

Then it was Len and Stan's turn for a bombshell. "We thought it would be a good idea to have a weekly interview with someone with an interesting life or story. We'll call it 'Down Your Street'. Liaise with Michael so that we can head it with a photo. You'll have to work with several weeks in hand so that there is no worry about the copy being ready in time."

Len and Stan exchanged glances; they seemed quite pleased, doubly so when Bill interjected that he had already jotted down a few names and they would start on them as soon as possible.

"Part of the page will have the fifty years ago bit so people will know where to look for it instead of it being dotted anywhere in the paper," God added. He looked at me. "Keep up the good work and get as many done as possible so that we can use them as fillers if any of the other copy is short."

Then he gave me the shock of my life. "You can write a column for women each week. Nothing too heavy; just get a few interviews with women who have done something and perhaps a few other stories to fill it up – about a quarter of a page we thought would be ideal."

I gulped, more or less inaudibly, I think. How was I going to find time for this, let alone dig up enough things for every week? Once again the sweetener was that I would get my name on the articles.

After the meeting, Bill took me aside. He had been primed by God to make everything sound simple. "We've been in contact with lots of PR people and you'll get handouts," he explained. "But you're not to let any advertising get in the paper since they won't have paid for it and they're just trying to get noticed." In one damning sentence, he dismissed the entire Public Relations industry.

He handed me a sheaf of printed matter. On the top was a recipe from the Potato Marketing Board for a dish which seemed to contain mainly mashed potato. Rifling through the pile, I saw I had publicity from everything which might possibly be of interest to females, from new cosmetics to knitting patterns. Yes, it was hopelessly stereotyped, but God and Bill knew that this was what housewives, the women of the fifties, would want to read. Career opportunities would not interest them, and we would not dare give advice on raising children or helping their education.

They'd produced a mocked-up page. My spot would be on the bottom quarter of the page with rather small type for the heading. 'This is the column women read, by Jen Hogarth,' it read. It seemed churlish to suggest that I might also like men to glance at this bit of the paper sometimes, and that my name was about quarter the size of Pete's and half that for the 'Down Your Street' bit shared by Len and Stan.

I spent most of the weekend worrying about how I was going to fill my space and decided that I must imagine a reader and write for her, which would help give the articles authority and purpose. So in my head, my only reader was 'Forty, fat and wanted to put her feet up'. What a pompous opinionated ass a teenager can be! But it must have worked, for over the next few years I had many complimentary letters and phone calls.

In the early weeks, I simply did not have enough to fill the space and stuck in a recipe for bread-and-butter pudding from the English Flour Board. It was an act of desperation, if I'm honest. I thought that not only would everyone know how to make bread-and-butter pudding, which was a staple in our household, but they could look it up in a recipe book if they wanted to make it.

How wrong I was. That week the letters flooded in with congratulations on what a good cook I was (in fact, at that point I had yet to make a bread-and-butter pudding myself) and could we print more recipes please? I showed these to Bill and we decided to save a lot of aggro by using a recipe most weeks as well as 'Household Hints', which were also popular. These I rewrote from an old *Pears Cyclopaedia*. I had no idea if they were any good or not, but again the letters came in, not just with praise but with other hints and homespun tips.

I approached Bill and we went together to God with the suggestion that the women's column should print readers' own recipes and hints; there would be no payment but contributors would see their names in print. "Good idea," he said gruffly. What a relief this was. If only I had had this brainwave when the column idea was first mooted.

I got in the habit, when I was out on any job for the paper, of looking for a local woman and approaching her for a chat. This quite often led to an article for my column. It was amazing what apparently ordinary women had done in the past, were currently doing or planned for the future. Among those I interviewed who particularly stood out were a nurse from the First World War who worked in France, an old lady who had been in Russia as a governess before the Revolution and another intrepid woman who drove alone in a baby Austin through various Balkan countries. She had taken phrase books with her to cope with the languages but had not realised that the AMO part of her number plate would lead to misunderstandings followed by hilarity.

One morning Bill called me into his room and told me he'd met a man in the pub the previous evening whose son had built a go-kart and was going to race it. I couldn't think what that had to do with me, or why I should be interested – I thought go-kart was just another name for a soap box on wheels which boys would knock up from a set of old pram wheels, bits of wood, with a bit of old rope to steer by.

"It's a new kind of motor racing," Bill explained. The father and son thought maybe a reporter could drive it round the practice dirt track they had constructed in the yard at the back of father's building business and write about the experience for a little exposure.

My jaw dropped. "But I can't drive!"

"It doesn't matter about a licence," said Bill. "You won't be on a public road. It doesn't have gears or brakes anyway. At the moment it's a bit of an experiment – let's call it a prototype – and you can write about it in your column."

It didn't seem to me that my readers were going to be any more interested in the project than I was. But the sub-editor just like the Editor had to be obeyed. So I called the builder and arranged to go the next afternoon when his son would be home from school.

It felt strange going to work in trousers when normally they were reserved for leisure. It did occur to me that it might be cold in the go-kart – like an open sports car, I assumed – so I wore a coat and took gloves and a head scarf.

Out in the yard was their home-made pride and joy. I can honestly say I'd never seen anything quite like it. It looked all engine and pipes and hardly any space to sit. The lad pulled on goggles and plunked himself in it. His dad got hold of a piece of cord, yanked, the engine roared to life and the whole contraption shook like a bad case of the DTs. Immediately he drove off around the oval track pursued by a cloud of black smoke. The man was explaining the go-kart's finer points to me but I couldn't hear a word until the lad was at the far end of the oval, and then he returned and speech was impossible again.

My ears were still ringing when they switched the engine off. The lad hopped out. His dad turned to me. "Your turn," he said brightly. As I arranged myself on the seat, I tried to ask sensible questions – like how do you stop – but he tugged the cord, the

Karting for the column: clearly minor safety considerations like a helmet or seat belt didn't enter the picture.

engine roared and I was off. It seemed a tremendous speed with the road showing between my feet, and cinders flying up. At the first corner I didn't so much guide it around as hang onto the steering wheel to stop being flung out. Were you supposed to lean into the corner as you did on a motor bike or a scooter? I'd been pillion on both, but once only, hating the noise, speed and general feeling that an accident was about to happen. I had my feet on pedals. I couldn't remember which was the accelerator and which the brake, only that I didn't want to go any faster. So I just lifted both feet into the air and luckily the engine cut out.

I was sipping a welcome mug extremely strong sweet tea in the hut that served as an office and trying to ask intelligent questions when moment Michael drew up in the van to take a picture of me. He had to settle for a 'still' as there was no way I was going to drive again. The photo and short article did appear in my column, but I never heard whether the lad and his kart progressed much beyond the cinder track.

It was far more interesting to meet a real racing driver, and a woman at that. I got an interview with Pat Moss, sister of Stirling, shortly after she and her co-driver won in the Monte Carlo Rally. My mouth fell open and pencil remained poised over the notebook when Stirling wandered into the room looking for something only to be unceremoniously shooed back out. Like all teenagers of the time, I would have loved to have been introduced to him, or even shaken his hand, but it was not to be. For once his sister was in the spotlight, not him.

She showed me the enormous glass vase which was the trophy they had won. She seemed quite full of herself, and probably with some justification: a cabinet at the house in Tring was full of the cups she'd won in equestrian competitions. "Thank goodness it's not more silverware to clean," was her comment.

IN THE LATE Fifties, the *Gazette*, the paper owned and edited by Mr Throg, suddenly appeared one week with a modern-looking front page. We were intrigued. It had been bumbling along with a regular readership and a good income from small advertisements. It had no rivals, as we had, and the loyal buyers who wanted to know what was happening in their immediate neighbourhood had no other way of finding out except by spending a modest sum and buying the paper on Tuesdays.

The *Gazette* was dull, dull, dull – in my opinion anyway. Mr Throg never rewrote anything. He had always printed in full any reports that were sent to his one-man office. He obviously read our paper every Friday and would lift large chunks of typeface directly to his paper if any of the people we wrote about lived in his area. If he was out reporting on the Assizes or Quarter Sessions in our county town, because one of his parishioners was up before the judge, he simply placed a 'Closed Today' notice on the door of the printing works and office. He did the same when he attended the Magistrates' Court. Something must have rocked his boat.

Then we heard that his nephew had gone to work for him. Our source of information was a reporter from our rival, the *Courier*, who had come across the young man at a parish council meeting where our boundaries coincided. He was full of the new reporter. "He had dark red corduroy trousers and a sports jacket and a cravat and Chelsea boots," he reported with awe in his voice.

This was significant. All the local male journalists wore dark off-the-peg suits with plain shirts and sombre ties; any derivation from this 'uniform' immediately brought criticism from the Editor and the comment that standards needed to be kept up. The only person at the *Herald* who could get away with a sports jacket was our sports editor. His concession was a well-worn number with leather patches at the elbows.

We younger reporters were having an illicit mid-morning Saturday coffee in a local cafe and hanging on to every word of the details of the new young reporter. "His name is Jeremy Throg," our informant continued. "Speaks in a rather Oxford accent. Says to call him Jerry."

We were keen to see Jerry in action and I didn't have to wait long. He turned up at a parish council meeting in the area where we both worked – a council that Mr Throg had never attended, relying instead on the minutes of the meeting being sent to him several weeks later by the parish clerk.

As an old hand, I had the agenda propped in front of me and whispered the relevant names of the four councillors and the chairman and clerk to this elegantly languid man at my side. In all other matters, I felt distinctly inadequate. I had a stubby pencil and the standard issue spiral-topped notebook; he had a slim fountain pen and a hardback book with blank ruled pages. I started with a few shorthand squiggles as the apologies were read out, and then listened to the minutes of the last meeting to get my head round what the council was likely to discuss. Jerry just wrote the name of the parish council in longhand.

While I and Mike, the *Courier* reporter, scribbled names in the margin and the gist of what the speakers had to say, Jerry sat with crossed legs and pen poised above his blank sheet of paper.

After the usual hour's circular discussion of items which had all been discussed before, the meeting closed. The only action voted on was an instruction that the clerk write a couple of letters. We shuffled out of the village hall. The lights of the local pub beckoned but I knew my last bus was due in ten minutes, while Mike had to go in the opposite direction on his bicycle.

But Jerry suggested a drink and even offered to run me the five miles home in his car. In the interests of getting information about him to relay to my friends and fellow reporters I accepted, and so did Mike.

As always, I opted for half a bitter shandy – the cheapest drink. Mike plumped for a pint rather than his usual half as Jerry was paying. Jerry ordered a gin and tonic for himself, a drink which I preferred but had long ago realised I could never request from colleagues or boy friends because it cost far too much.

We sat at a table. It was bliss not to have to gulp the drink down in order to get the bus.

Jerry held the floor, telling us about Oxford University and his degree and how he was going to modernise his uncle's paper, giving him practical experience before he headed for a prestigious job in Fleet Street. In his drawling voice, it did not sound arrogant, just that he was confident and knew exactly what direction his life was going to take. He even smelt different from other young men of my acquaintance. There was a strong odour of aftershave and none of cigarettes.

He asked us if we were on the new national training scheme for journalists which led to a certificate – the only qualification available. Mike explained that his editor had been approached but refused to allow any of his staff the day off a week they would need to go to the local college. I had never even heard of the

National Council for the Training of Journalists and made a mental note to get hold of the literature.

When I did, I found like Mike that the council only offered training to someone already employed in journalism. The rather stuffy booklet stating how the scheme worked, explaining "it should be understood at the outset that the industry's representatives, through the National Council, have repeatedly affirmed that all trainees should acquire the basic skills of the reporter, including shorthand. Thus too early specialisation (for instance on the sub-editors' or sports desks, and in the case of girls, on women's page topics) may well be a handicap to young journalists seeking to pass the Council's Proficiency Certificate." In my eyes, that meant I was not eligible so I only skimmed through the rest of the booklet.

JERRY WAS an erratic driver and obviously considered his souped up old banger was equivalent to a racing car, so I never accepted another lift from him. But he was having far more impact on his uncle's paper. He often gave himself a byline and the headlines extended over three or more columns. 'Special articles' started appearing in the *Gazette*, included a weekly piece of no local interest from 'Our Air Correspondent'. This was the title they gave to a retired RAF Air Marshal who lived locally and near to Mr Throg. His main claim to fame, as far as I could tell, was that at Armistice Day he always had the most medals clanking on his chest and, because of seniority, led the parade.

Through Jerry's ideas, the Throgs had obviously rounded up a great many local dignitaries and convinced them to contribute. There was even 'Our Correspondent in America', the daughter of the WI president who had been a GI bride after the war. The family farmed somewhere unknown in the Midwest. Her articles were just plain boring, though we did envy the deep freeze and the big television she wrote about.

Curiously, even the very mundane reports, such as whist drives, were divided into sections in the *Gazette*. The first bit was labelled NEWS. Well. Was I missing something or did everyone else also assume that was what one would read in a newspaper? But then there was the next paragraph tagged COMMENT which might contain the inadvisable suggestion that the winners were the same as the previous weekly report. Some items, including parish council meetings, had a third segment labelled BACKGROUND. I felt Jerry was probably alienating more readers than he was winning over with his brand of modernising, but maybe we were just not ready for it. Maybe the *Herald* as well as all the other locals could do with this sort of new writing.

But then there was the week when the new-look *Gazette* led with a large headline on the front page: IMPORTANT ROMAN DISCOVERY. Our dismay at missing a major story quickly turned to incredulity and then fits of laughter when we saw that they had fallen for the oldest cod trick in journalism.

The paper had received a letter from a Mr Ivor Peter Standing, and even printing it with initials in the style of the paper – I P Standing – had not rung any alarm bells with Jerry or his uncle.

'Mr Standing' wrote that he was a farmer and in ploughing some waste ground had made an important discovery of pottery. He had washed the broken pieces and when put together he found some Latin words and hoped that the *Gazette* could translate them, and suggest whether the pottery had any monetary value as farming was very depressed and he could do with a new plough.

He had written out the inscription in capital letters, and the *Gazette* duly obliged by printing it, in a large Times Roman (appropriately) type face on its front page:

ITI SAPIS SPOTANDAU SEDONE.

We stared in astonishment and fell about laughing as, with quick strokes of his blue pencil, Bill changed the spaces: IT IS A PISS POT AND A USED ONE.

Immediately Bill was lifting the phone. "This one's mine!" he said almost threateningly as he dialled the number of a subs desk on the raciest paper in Fleet Street.

The headline story in the next issue of the *Gazette* told a very different story. It had been purchased by an evening newspaper based in Oxford and would be closing its local office.

Jerry did phone me at home to say he was going to New York to try his luck and I wished him well. But Mr Throg, his whiskers, and another tweed suit were still to be seen on a bar stool every evening in the local hostelry he patronised. He made a reasonable income by getting his former local correspondents (not the special ones Jerry had instigated) to give him the usual scruffy bits of paper with the results of football matches, the reports of local fetes and festivities. He forwarded them to the office in Oxford and was paid lineage.

But local reading habits were hard to change. Few people bothered to buy the evening paper that tried to replace the *Gazette*, even though it said it would contain news and adverts from their area. In fact, I think the *Herald* picked up more than it did on Mr Throg's home patch.

– 8 –

CATCHING THE NEWS

TODAY'S NEWS IS a bit like fast food: we expect it delivered hot, quickly and to our taste – and as soon as it's consumed, it's history and usually forgotten. It saddens me to see news turned into just another throw-away commodity and journalists hitting rock-bottom on the list of people the public trusts.

Sixty or more years ago, life was much more sedate, giving those of us recording its ups and downs in the pages of our newspapers time to think. Probably our methods of getting the news hadn't changed much since the days of the Pony Express in the Wild West. Where they carried mail and papers from stage to stage on horseback, we used buses, trains and pedal cycles and the telephone wherever possible.

Of course there were no mobile phones; we used public telephone kiosks, so an essential part of every reporter's equipment was two old pence – the cost of a call. There were telegrams, but the cost per word was exorbitant if anything more than a short note was required. Letters would reach their destination overnight; this, believe it or not, was the quickest and most reliable form of getting news reports.

It seems hard to imagine now, but cars back then were the preserve of the fortunate, and impecunious young reporters were happy to accept lifts in whatever vehicle was going our way: cars, trucks, vans, hearses, and occasionally a police Wolsey with their real leather brown seats and running boards.

Usually, when I was stranded in a remote district, there were one or two other reporters and we would start walking, turning hopefully every time we heard a vehicle approaching. Most people stopped. There was far less traffic on the country roads, and motorists didn't think that a couple of young people were going to steal their car and we certainly did not expect every driver to be a murderer or rapist.

The police weren't supposed to give us lifts. Many policemen themselves still had to rely on pushbikes or – the more fortunate – low-powered motorcycles. So it was exciting, after a long day in a district Magistrates' Court, when young constables asked me how I was getting back to Aylesbury and offered me an illicit lift.

The odd times that happened, I had to start walking away from the town in case any official saw them leave with a passenger. The police car would follow me, stop, and I would hop in the back and ride royally until we approached Aylesbury and I had to get out. If it was raining, they were usually kind and let me lie along the back seat so no one would know they had a passenger. They would let me out in a quiet back street.

Another fairly regular lift was far more overt. The local coroner was also head of a well-established and very old-fashioned solicitor's practice in town. Mr Wilkinson had played golf with my father and I had known him since I was a child. However, he was an absolute stickler for proprieties. He still wore a stiff wing collar with a black three-piece suit when he officiated at inquests.

Usually inquests were held at various hospitals, but occasionally they would be at the home of the deceased or a village hall. Once I was the only reporter at a remote farmhouse for the inquest of a farmer who had come to an untimely end due to not understanding a new piece of equipment. It was too far to cycle and Michael had grudgingly taken me there, but would not wait for the inquest to end. Anyway, he reasoned, I had my contacts in the police and was fairly certain of a return lift. But the coroner's officer and other officials were all from another area and I couldn't recognise anyone who might help me get back home.

In those days, we never ever thought of getting a taxi. First, it would be a case of finding a phone; then, taxis only operated from the railway station and it would be very expensive to get one to drive many miles for one passenger.

When Mr Wilkinson found out that I would probably have thumbed a lift, he was horrified and offered me the first of his many lifts. "I shall have to have words with Mr Godber," he exclaimed in high dudgeon. "He should not send well brought up girls like you to my little hearings. They ought to be just male reporters."

"Oh no," I begged. "Please don't. We get equal pay, you see, so I have to do anything."

But actually I did agree with him. The way some people meet their end can be fairly gruesome even when it is described in the clinical calm and hush of coroners' court. The worst was when children had been killed, and it was so hard to be detached and not shed a tear at the distress of the parents or witnesses. I would stare hard at the notebook and try not to let emotion take over. Young reporters have feelings, and I would hear the youths blowing their noses hard and quietly wiping eyes just like me.

So I followed Mr Wilkinson out to the yard. His gleaming old Bentley was parked on the baked mud where the cows crossed twice daily on their way to be milked. A black limousine seemed out of place amid broken machinery, rusty tractors and an all-purpose Land Rover with no windows and a canvas top, but that's what he drove.

With old-fashioned courtesy he opened a passenger door at the rear of the car and ushered me in. "I'm sorry but you must ride in the back seat. In my position, I cannot be compromised in any way. I'm sure you understand."

So I was chauffeur-driven home.

It was even more embarrassing one December evening when it was almost dark and once again I was in the back seat, but the courtesy light in the centre of the car roof had to remain on all the time. This was just in case anyone should recognise his car and there would be absolutely no chance of any hanky-panky with the young lady as she was safely ensconced in the back and would not have the opportunity to compromise his good name in any way.

I noticed in the course of that first lift home that we seemed to proceed at a very stately speed down the country road. There was no other traffic. I peeped between the back seats and saw that the speedometer needle appeared to be stuck on thirty miles an hour. It never varied, even around corners, and I began to think that it was broken, although such a law-abiding citizen would surely get it mended immediately. However, as we approached the thirty-mile speed limit signs at the outskirts of Aylesbury, the needle dropped to twenty-five. No way was he going to break the speed limit. But the trouble was it never dropped any lower until we suddenly braked for some traffic lights.

Later, by way of explanation, his clerk told me that Mr Wilkinson had learned to drive during the First World War. Of course he had never taken a driving test but had a licence by default. Apparently it was very difficult to change gear in his car, and so by keeping a steady speed he could remain in top all the time. Since he was the senior partner in his law firm as well as being the coroner, all the local police knew his car and never stopped him. It was long before the days of MOTs, and I suspect his ancient sedan with its running boards and large mascot on the front would not be roadworthy today.

THE RAMIFICATIONS of all these challenges of communication and transportation arrangements meant that we had to plan our efforts very carefully. Usually you had one chance to get your story and if you didn't, you were snookered, or worse still, scooped by the opposition. Mind you, there are few professional achievements as satisfying as getting your own scoop, especially if it was the result of a carefully planned and executed campaign, like the one I was involved in.

Our main competition was the *Courier*. We had to use guile and ingenuity to beat them. They were part of a newspaper chain with greater resources and far bigger printing presses. The *Courier* was published the day after us and usually, annoyingly, lifted great chunks of stories from us and regurgitated them with the minimum of re-writing. We took a dim view of this, derided their methods as lazy and unprofessional, but of course could do nothing about it.

Coming out a day before the opposition gave us the advantage of being first with most stories, but when something big happened on our press day, all we could do was sit back and fume as they sold all the copies they could print. It was most galling when the big story was predictable, happened year after year, and the *Courier* always profited.

Every autumn, there was a big agricultural show on the boundaries of our circulation area, at Old Amersham, but it attracted all the farming community and the reports were read avidly to see who had won what. Because of our deadline and having to 'go to bed' on the day of the show, all we could do was write a general article and keep our fingers crossed that the show took place and hadn't been struck by a plague of locusts. By the time our long report detailing all the prize-winners appeared the following week, everyone had already read about it – in the *Courier*.

But one year God and Bill devised a devilish plan. All the reporters were summoned to a meeting, the plan was explained and we were all sworn to secrecy. If it worked, it would be a masterstroke worthy of a top military tactician – God liked that idea – and we would succeed for once in scooping the *Courier* and racking up bumper sales of our paper.

On the day of the show, Pete and Len left by train for Amersham early in the morning as usual. It was the same train that the *Courier* reporters caught. It would be fair to describe them as a smug bunch that day. Perfect.

Once at the showground, which was in the grounds of a crumbling stately home called Shardeloes – since restored – reporters and photographers were really out on a limb. It's hard to imagine today that the showground had no direct telephone line, but that's the way it was. None of the organisers could think why one should be required when contingencies were in place for every eventuality. The St John Ambulance was always in attendance for any medical emergencies and so was a veterinary team, for the animals being shown were far more valuable than any members of the public who paid to attend. The local fire brigade always had an engine on display too among the stalls of the exhibitors by the parade ring. There never had been a fire but they were there in case of an emergency. The only time I remember them doing anything was on a very hot summers' day at a show I attended when some of the pigs got distressed in the heat and had to be hosed down.

On this day, Pete was carrying his own portable typewriter – in itself a first: he never used his portable for work; typical leftie, he insisted that all the tools for his trade were provided by the management. He wrote his stories in the office after touring the showground.

Normally our team had to leave the show shortly before lunch in order to get the stopping train back, while our rival reporters remained until nearly the end. God always lived in fear that he would be a laughing stock if our paper carried the story that the show had been a great success when it fact it had been rained off. Of course, our competition longed for the day when there might be an earthquake or thunderstorm so they could lead their reports with something dramatic.

The forced early exit was one of our team's perpetual grumbles, not because they feared missing a big story but because this was the best free meal of the day. Before the days of hospitality tents, reporters were lucky to get a plate of dry sandwiches, which was what normally happened at the other agricultural shows we covered around the region. But this county show had a reputation to uphold. The president entertained guests with a full three-course meal and plenty of drink; members of the press were permitted to sit at a table to the rear of the tent. You could tell which table was ours: the one from which the bottles had been removed. The wine was for the show's guests, after all – but there was still a free drink for us and a plate of cold salmon with salad and strawberries and cream to follow.

This particular year, the team was able to enjoy the lunch, take advantage of a short interview with the president, and watch some of the events in the main ring as well as copying out all the results. The lists of the prize-winners, whether they were cattle or vegetables, showjumpers or dogs, were handwritten and there was only one copy. They were usually pinned to the central pole in the press tent, which was an old army surplus job that looked like it might have done service at Mafeking.

There was a bit of banter about our team missing the train and also that the reports would all be a week late in the issue after next. But Pete and Len took the teasing in good spirit and kept their mouths shut.

The station was a brisk walk uphill. Most of the reporters followed the crowds to the platform for trains going south and towards London. Probably nobody noticed Pete and Len waiting on the other platform, and if they did, they would have made light of it as another *faux pas* by the hapless *Herald* hacks. When the steam express, the Master Cutler non-stop to Sheffield pulled in, they boarded it.

My role in the scoop was very humble, but absolutely vital to its success. Some time before the Master Cutler was due to roar straight through Aylesbury station, I had purchased a platform ticket for a penny, crossed over the bridge and taken up a position beside the track. I waited in some trepidation, very nervous that the great plan was going to be a fiasco and it would all be my fault.

I could hear the lines vibrating before I saw the monster engine bearing down fast. About halfway along, I could see an open window and a man leaning out. As he passed, a bundle of copy came hurling towards me – and I literary caught the news.

There was just time to see Len giving a thumbs-up from behind Pete before they and the train had disappeared into the distance. But a porter, idly leaning against his trolley in the sunshine, had seen me beside the train and was now running down the platform. "What are you doing?" he yelled, shaken from his stupor. "You can't take delivery of goods like that! They have to go in the guard's van, you know. This is not a stopping train. Everything in it is going to Sheffield."

But I had a head start on him and was running over the bridge clasping the precious parcel, and savouring the drama of the moment.

Back at the office, Bill rapidly scanned the copy, breaking up the various stories, and writing the headlines and cross-heads. Within minutes, God was nodding his approval and the linotype operators were busy setting the type while the printers got the headlines ready.

The stone had a big gap for this front-page story (although

photographs would have to wait until the next week when the plates were developed and the blocks made). Finally the foreman and head printer were able to drop in the large letters of type for the splash headline and we all stood back to relish the moment. We had thoroughly scooped our rivals. The print run would be extended to many more copies of the paper to give the local farming community what they wanted: the names of who had won the cups and prizes and all the results in the small print.

On Friday morning, we were still reading our paper and congratulating ourselves when two bleary-eyed and unshaven men rolled into the office. Poor Pete and Len had had to spend the night sleeping in the carriage which was in the sidings at Sheffield in order to catch the first stopping train back in the morning. Their plan had been to find a bed and breakfast, but both had fallen asleep in the train and been shunted with it into the siding.

I got congratulations all round too: my excellent catch and sprint escape was a real talking point. "You scooped up that parcel of copy to give us the scoop of the year," Pete said. After the excitement of our cloak-and-dagger operation, it was back to writing obituaries and weddings and reporting on meetings and garden fetes. But it was nice to have the *Courier* reporters treating us with a new respect, not to say active suspicion.

FLEET STREET FANTASIES

EVERY REPORTER in our office had the impossible dream that something sensational would happen on our patch; they would get the story and flog it to the national dailies and in so doing make a name for themselves, plus a small fortune by our standards. Most important in this version of The Dream, they would make a name for themselves and Fleet Street would bombard them with offers of permanent employment on a vastly inflated salary.

The more prosaic version of the dream (the lower case version) was to get in somebody's black book as their regional stringer. This mostly meant filing local stories that were strong enough to make a paragraph or two in the daily but not important enough for a London reporter to be sent to the scene. Stories that made it brought in a few welcome extra pounds.

The senior reporters and Bill all had the papers that paid the most - the *Mirror*, the *Daily Sketch* and the *News of the World* – and jealously guarded these contacts. Then as now, the more salacious the story, the greater the chance of having it picked up. Scandal of any sort had pound signs attached, although sex and sleaze had to be handled carefully then rather than blatantly as now.

I had *Dog World*. I got it after a local breeder of boxer dogs died. I was writing his obituary and the paper got a phone call from the editor asking for a short report on the funeral. It was not one that we would normally have attended but I managed to find time to get there and submitted a list of mourners (and the various breeds of dogs they represented) together with a short obituary and so earned a handy extra sum. It strikes me as strange, even now, that the breeders were keener on having the breed of their dog after their names rather than whether they knew the deceased, but presumably that was what mattered in their world.

If *Dog World* was a surprise, the next approach was positively jaw-dropping. It was *The Times*. I hasten to add the job came my way by default although I like to think there was at least a little merit involved. God was their stringer but had to relinquish the role on a technicality. They wrote to him and said that it was now imperative that their local correspondent could be accessed by phone twenty-four hours a day, not just in office hours. None of the other reporters had one, and neither did the Editor. This was partly because of the shortage of telephone lines for many years after the war. But we were on the telephone at home. Because of my father's work during the war, we had always been able to have a telephone. He had been heavily involved in the reorganisation of a country at war, overseeing evacuation of children from cities and moving hospitals, medical staff and patients from London.

Automatic dialling hadn't come to our area, and didn't until some time later, either. You lifted your receiver off the hook and waited until someone at the telephone exchange responded. The ladies at the exchange knew (or thought they knew) what was going on the community by virtue of who was phoning whom. When I gave the number for a friend whose father was a doctor, the lady at the exchange – Hilda, who was also the local postmistress – always said, "The doctor's out. Do you want me to take a message?" Then I had to explain it was a personal call.

Everybody knew that under-worked telephone operators in rural areas nearly always listened in to calls through boredom. You could sometimes hear the click of knitting needles as she said, "I'm putting you through." There would be a pause, then a click and the voice would trill, "You're through."

When Hilda learned that I was a reporter on the *Herald*, she would sometimes ring through to the office and ask for me. She would then repeat some scurrilous and quite unprintable story that she had overheard while working on the telephone switchboard. Today she could have made her fortune as a stringer, or even as a blackmailer. Or landed behind bars for invasion of privacy.

The upshot of the new edict from *The Times* meant that God could no longer take any freelance work from the Old Thunderer. Personally I thought *The Times* was over-rated. It still covered its front page with small advertisements – often very intriguing ones in the personal column – with news starting on the first inside page. Its headlines were small, but the columns of print gave news with far more detail and accuracy than you find today with the trend of instant analysis and stories forgotten by the next day.

So I now had the kudos of being 'Our Correspondent' for *The Times of London*. I thought it was a big honour, but Father said he hoped they were not going to wake him up by ringing in the night. "And if you're going to be on the phone to London from home, you'll either have to reverse the charges or pay me for the call," he told me sternly. How mobile phones have revolutionised communication and its cost.

At first I was thrilled when either a letter (if the story wasn't urgent) or a phone call came from *The Times* with a job for me. Pete would alter the diary so that I could attend or get the report. It was usually something dreary like the annual meeting of the local hunt or a local bigwig getting a promotion.

Then I would phone through my copy and the next day see not my name in print, but the small paragraph I had submitted and under the headline, From Our Own Correspondent. If I sent the paper a story of my own, it would appear with the byline From Our Special Correspondent. But it was still a thrill. I rather mixed up special agents and special correspondents in my mind, but it didn't lead to any offers of jobs.

Nor did the time the back of my head appeared on every paper one Monday morning.

Chequers, the Prime Minister's country house, was not far from where we lived. There was great excitement in the locality when US President Eisenhower and his wife were to pay a private weekend visit there. Obviously it wasn't really private; he was in London for talks with Harold Macmillan, the Tory Prime Minister, and the British Government.

When the Prime Minister had weekend guests at Chequers, they often went to church with him on Sunday morning at the small local parish church in Ellesborough. This was on the schedule for Ike and Mamie, as the tabloids were fond of calling the Eisenhowers. As chief reporter, Pete chose himself as the reporter assigned a seat in the press pews. Michael was obviously scheduled to take the pictures, and Bill thought it would be a good idea to have a reporter in the crowds by the church to get a few quotes on the reactions of the locals. That was me.

For once we didn't mind giving up our Sunday morning for the job. We had to get to Ellesborough early because there was very little parking in the area. So after Michael had parked the van, we helped get him and his camera into a good viewpoint near the church's lych-gate. Pete showed his ticket to the lone policeman in the church porch and was ushered inside.

We waited and waited for the President of the United States to arrive; the bells pealed and the villagers craned forward to see Ike the war hero and now president – but he didn't appear. There was a back entrance from Chequers. It dawned on us that they'd used this to get the cars from there to a manor house next to the

Eisenhower, Macmillan and the cottage whose garden 'donated' the roses.

church and to usher the official party in at the rear of the church, away from public gaze. However, the buzz went round that they would walk down the path after the service to the car waiting at the lych-gate.

This was the first time that I had seen Fleet Street photographers en masse. Most had stepladders, sharp elbows and no compunction about treading on graves to get the best viewpoint. Poor Michael was continually jostled and hustled and kept losing his place at the front of the pack.

A crackly loudspeaker was broadcasting the service to those waiting outside. I'd spoken to various people in the crowd about how they felt about the visit of the President of the United States of America to their village and church, and had what I hoped Pete would want to use (and I had remembered to get all the local names and their initials for their moment of fame next week when their comments could appear in the local paper.)

Just as we got to the final hymn, Michael rushed past me while I was waiting on the edge of the path. He dashed into the nearby cottage garden where the owner and friends were waiting by the gate. I'd spoken to them earlier. As regular churchgoers and long-time residents, they were furious that they had been turned away from the service through lack of space.

Without pausing a second, Michael approached the rose bush which had pride of place in the centre of the lawn and wrenched off some blooms. There was a bit of an outcry but he yelled, "Can't stop now. I'll come back and explain later." He pushed his way back and beckoned to me. "Stand next to me and when the President gets nearly to the lych-gate, rush forward and give him the roses. Then he'll stop and I can get a good picture."

"Great idea man," said one of the American press pack, his neck hung with cameras. "Get the little lady to stop him and we'll all get good pix."

He thrust the roses at me. I tried to make them look like a bouquet but the petals were crushed and the stems broken. So I broke one off and decided to try and put it in the President's buttonhole, which would make him stop a moment while the cameras clicked.

The American photographer nudged me. "You say in a loud voice, 'English rose from an English rose, sir'."

What a cringe-making line. No, I couldn't. I had to think of something else.

But at that moment, the loudspeakers boomed out a most peculiar panting noise. I knew that it was the boy who pumped the bellows for the organ getting the air into it prior to the crash of the opening chords of the hymn. The Americans looked startled. They weren't to know, as we did, that village churches couldn't afford to get electricity to power their organs, so they used a succession of muscular lads to provide the power by hand-pumping the bellows. Plus it usually drowned out the officiating clergyman's final words.

Soon the door of the church opened. A policeman was stationed on each side of it and the local vicar led his distinguished congregation out. Prime Minister Macmillan was escorting Mrs Eisenhower and it looked like a couple of security men next followed by the President and Mrs Macmillan. Mamie Eisenhower had chosen a peculiar hat like a flat pancake while Mrs Macmillan was dressed in her usual tweed suit with a sensible felt hat.

We clapped as the first of the procession passed us and then my moment came. I stepped forward just after the bodyguards passed and handed the President my rose. He looked a little startled and took the rose without a word. There was lots of clapping so I didn't have any awkward silences to fill with an inane comment; I didn't have to say anything and no one assumed that I might have a knife hidden in the flower or that I had stopped the President in order that someone could get a gun out. No, it was very civilised and after he had left the churchyard, he dropped the rose in the gutter as he got in the limousine. And the next morning there was the back of my anonymous head in the papers. No one printed my name, thank goodness, and even the people at the cottage seemed quite pleased that their rose had been presented to the President.

MOST OF my friends had little interest in politicianss, war heroes or not. They were more interested in Hollywood film stars. A few minor celebrities lived in our area, in relative obscurity. One I met was an actress whom I'll call Sally Westfield. She had been famous twenty or so years earlier for her appearances in farces in London's West End. Admittedly I had never heard of her but my informant was certain that she would agree to be interviewed for my Women's Page at the remote country cottage she and her current husband had recently purchased. Without the Internet, research was much more difficult than it is today. I had looked in the library to try and find out something about Miss Westfield – but there was only a list of the roles she had played and they meant nothing to me.

We arranged a date and time over the telephone and as a photograph would be essential, I could get a ride there with Michael. The cottage took a long time to find as it was down several unmarked lanes and through a water splash. It was the typical English chocolate box cottage – thatched roof sagging down over the tiny leaded light windows, a riot of roses round the porch, a white painted wooden gate and a stream burbling just past the entrance.

Sally and her husband must have heard the van coming and were waiting for us, artfully posed in the doorway. They certainly knew what would make a good picture, and it did: Michael took that shot before we left – and sold it a good many times in the years to come.

We were ushered into the dark interior of a poky sitting room, which led straight off the entrance, and coffee was served. I can't remember her husband's name because Sally dominated the conversation with lots of noisy gesticulation; her wrists were covered in silver charm bracelets that tinkled as she waved her arms theatrically. "Have you been to any of my plays?" she asked.

I had to confess I hadn't (anyway, I would have been only a baby at the height of her fame). So out came the scrapbooks, and I was able to jot down some facts to go with the stream of chatter and reminiscences that she was giving me. I realised Miss Westfield had never been the leading lady, but fame had struck because she appeared on the London stage in peach silk camiknickers – very daring and possibly a little scandalous at the time. It was that, not her acting abilities, for which she was known.

Sally told me that she and her new husband (they had only recently married and I was not to mention either of their previous liaisons) had decided to retire and live a life of bliss in the country. Reading between the lines, I realised that both were past their sell-by date, probably couldn't get parts and the money was drying up – hence the move to this rural backwater.

The interview over and the picture taken, we jolted back down the lanes. The article with its photograph duly appeared some weeks later.

That November, the weather became stormy; it rained and rained just as it had over the Coronation some years before in the summer, and Sally and her husband floated back into the news – literally. The little stream by their idyllic cottage became a miniature torrent complete with rapids. Not only did it overflow, it swamped the ground floor of the cottage. We got the story from the fire brigade who were supposed to be pumping out, but the lane was so narrow their appliance couldn't reach the cottage.

Michael parked the van some distance away, donned wellingtons and managed to get to the cottage where the bedraggled pair were pulling ruined furniture and wet belongings out and heaping them on what had been the front garden among the litter from the roses blown down by the stormy winds. Both Sally and her husband looked exhausted and haggard but did agree to have a photograph taken in the same spot where Michael had shot them on our earlier visit.

Michael earned a lot when the two photos – a sort of fairy tale before and a nightmare after – appeared side by side in national Sunday newspapers, together with the hard luck story that the cottage had been uninsurable because the stream was so close. This was followed by the pair appearing 'exclusively' (together with Michael's pictures) in a number of true life and confession magazines, which earned them enough to clear their debts and retire to yet another idyllic life – this time in France long before it became popular with expats.

For some years, Sally sweetly sent me Christmas cards with flowery messages and lots of exclamation marks, and always including an invitation to visit, probably assuming that I would never manage to do that. She was right; I never did.

IN OUR small country town and rural backwater, I seldom had the opportunity to meet the great and famous, but I did manage one interview that all my male colleagues would have killed to do.

It happened by complete chance. There had been a lot of traffic in the Market Square and a great many people milling around. Rumour had it that it was a film crew and some scenes were to be shot round the war memorial. Someone called in at the newspaper office with the tip-off and Len was despatched to cover the story.

It was a quiet day in the office, so when I had finished all my rewrites and Pete could not produce any more, I asked if I could go and see what was going on. "Take Michael with you," he said. "Maybe this film has some big stars."

We walked up the road and saw that the crowds were still there. It took a while to find Len who was chatting to some other local press. It was all very boring, he told us; no one knew what was happening.

Michael and I decided to go to a cafe off the square for a cup of coffee. It was actually one of our favourite places for skiving. It had been an old cottage; the rooms were heavily beamed and one led off from another like a rabbit warren. We walked through the first room aiming for our usual snug at the back where we would be safe from anyone wanting to talk to us. But the door was shut and two large gentlemen in very tight and shiny black suits were loitering nearby.

"Excuse me," I said politely as I tried to pass.

"No go in," said the larger of the two in very heavily accented English.

Then his pal noticed the camera round Michael's neck. "You take pictures?"

"Yes, we're from the press," I said rather brashly, and hunted in my handbag to produce my notepad.

One of the men sidled through the door and I could hear a rapid exchange, possibly in Italian, possibly Spanish, but certainly foreign. "Okay, you come," he beckoned. "But only five minute before we film."

The second man stood aside for us and there, sitting at a table drinking coffee, was the most famous Italian film star of the day, Sophia Loren.

I was genuinely taken aback. She was even more beautiful than in her films. I was so amazed that it was easy to be a gushing

It was hard not to be a gushing fan face to face with Sophia Loren.

fan and say how much I enjoyed her films. Luckily she spoke halting English with a fascinating accent since my knowledge of Italian was zero and I was still in a state of shock to be actually in the same room as her. Her male companion was more fluent in English – certainly more so than the two wrestlers on the door. I tried to think of questions to ask her but she was more interested in asking about England and where she was as it was her first visit.

More coffee arrived. I didn't ask the right questions, about her film or about anything really that would add up to the kind of publicity that obviously her manager was seeking. It pains me to admit this once-in-a-lifetime opportunity quickly descended into two girls giggling as we compared the colour of our nail varnish and the bother when it chipped. She offered me a cigarette and lit one herself. The picture Michael took shows her smoking with impossible elegance.

All too soon there was a knock on the door and she was called to start filming. But we had our small scoop and went back to the office, forgetting about poor Len who spent most of the day hanging around with little in the way of a story.

I wanted my piece and the picture for my column, but no, it was splashed on the front page the following week, a great photo of a gorgeous star in conversation with someone who, naturally, was blanked out. I had to fill the column with recipes yet again – though possibly my readers would not have been as enamoured with Sophia Loren as I was.

ROBERT MAXWELL was in every respect the opposite of La Loren: bullying, arrogant and coarse. He was at the beginning of his short parliamentary career and standing in Buckingham constituency as the Labour candidate.

In the run-up to the General Election, Pete had a list of all the candidates and their meetings. I was down to cover an early evening meeting for Mr Maxwell at a local village hall. Unfortunately I was the only member of the press there; my colleagues from the other papers had given it a miss. In fact, I think there were only half a dozen members of the public present, including the chairman's wife and Mr Maxwell's agent. I scribbled a few notes to show I was paying attention. Luckily the meeting looked like it was going to be short so I would be home early. But Mr Maxwell had other ideas.

He first of all asked me which paper I represented and told his agent to be sure to get a copy next week. Then he asked me if I was going on to his next meeting.

"Er, no," I replied. "We have to be fair and cover the same number of meetings for each candidate."

"Of course, of course, I understand that. But the next venue is bigger so I am giving a speech with much more content. I'll give you a lift."

I remembered from Pete's list that the next meeting was nearer home so I wouldn't have so far to walk and surely I could listen to him again and just elaborate my notes a bit more. I went outside with the agent and we started walking down the street. "The car's along here," he commented. "It's not far." I wondered why they hadn't used the half-empty car park outside the hall.

Down a side street, I could see a big car parked. It was a beautiful Rolls-Royce. I could hear Mr Maxwell's footsteps behind us and as we approached, the chauffeur got out to open the door. Mr Maxwell indicated that I should ride in the rear with him and the agent got in the front.

The smell of the pristine cream leather was heady, the seat was so comfortable and the engine so quiet that I had not realised we had even started to glide away. All too soon we were at the village where the next meeting was to be held. Once again we drove past the hall and at the instruction of the agent, the chauffeur turned into a small lane and parked. Mr Maxwell turned round to the back shelf and took down a tweed cap, which he put on and adjusted to a jaunty angle. "You go with him," he said, nodding towards his agent. "I'll be along in a moment."

Having been brought up to be polite, I started to thank him for the lift but with an imperious wave of his hand he shooed me away.

We got to the hall and this time there were a couple of others at the press table as well as a few more members of the public. The chairman had obviously started the meeting and was now able to say, "Here comes our splendid candidate, soon to be our Member of Parliament," and everyone stood up to clap as Robert Maxwell in his working man's cap strode down between the rows of wooden chairs. He put his cap on the table in front of him and proceeded to give exactly the same speech as before. My colleagues were intrigued to see that I was just writing the words over my shorthand notes. When it got to "any questions?" I stood up and tiptoed out of the hall.

But my early exit had been noted and the next time Mr Maxwell met me, he used it to my disadvantage. This was some months later; he had not been elected on his first venture into politics although he was soon afterwards. The local trade unions were holding a conference – on a Sunday. When the date was put in the Bible, we all read it and hoped the job would go to someone else. No one wanted to work on Sundays.

But of course I saw that my initials had been put down beside it. I gathered up a great wodge of papers from the box next to the Bible, which had all the subjects which were going to be covered at the conference. I did mention to Pete that I could easily write it up from all this information. "Do I have to go?" I begged. "I could phone the organiser on Monday and confirm numbers and that all the speakers had turned up."

But no, apparently the owner of our paper had decided that we were being too Conservative Blue and must give equal coverage to the Liberals and the Labour Party.

So, not in the best of moods, I walked down to the hall on a beautiful sunny day when my friends had invited me to join them for a game of tennis and couldn't understand that I not only had to go to a trade union conference, but had to be there at the beginning.

Actually I was about ten minutes late because I had some new shoes with very high heels and I had not allowed enough time to walk to the hall. I opened the door as quietly as I could and heard Mr Maxwell's voice welcoming the delegates and outlining the plans for the day. I stood just inside the door behind the rows of seats. I saw that the press table was right at the front under the stage and recognised a couple of faces.

Then a booming voice said, "Come down here, sister."

The stiletto heels clattered alarmingly on the wooden floor however carefully I tried not to make a noise. Heads swivelled to see who was coming. Face bright red, I tried to sidle into position behind the press table when he leaned over and said,

"You're late, sister. I was just welcoming the sisters and brothers."

It made me want to giggle because I thought his manner of address sounded more like nuns and monks than political representatives. Mr Maxwell persisted. "Why are you late?"

"I've been to communion, sir, and needed to have some breakfast afterwards before coming here," I whispered.

That got him off my back. He cleared his throat and began his speech again. It was all very boring and we passed notes at the press table, and decided that we wouldn't come back after the coffee break. Like me, two of the other young reporters were furious at having to work because they belonged to football teams and were missing their games.

Maxwell didn't win that time, or the next, but he kept putting himself forward, and the Labour Party kept nominating him, and eventually in 1964 he was elected to the Commons. I expect he was insufferable after that. He lasted six years until his defeat in 1970. When Maxwell died in mysterious circumstances so many years later, and the full details emerged of his systematic looting of Mirror Group pension funds, I remembered his cynical 'working man' act with even greater distaste.

MY THEATRICAL sparring partner, Nigel Clavering, turned up again at one of the Young Conservative meetings where the speaker had been even duller than usual. He and I and several others left the hall and went to the local pub in search of a more convivial evening. The banter was good, we had a drink and an altogether better time than the Young Tories had offered. Toward the end of the evening, he asked me if I would like to go for tea at his home the next Sunday. I wasn't doing anything else and so I agreed. He was pleasant enough and the experience of acting opposite him had actually been fun, to be honest. He was to come and pick me up at my house. Despite the fact that I was out of my teens and going all over the place and often late at night for the *Herald*, my parents still expected me to bring any dates home for vetting, and anyway, since I didn't know where he lived, it was going to be easier to be driven there.

Father was off playing golf, but Mother gave the lanky young man in his sports jacket with leather patches the once over. After a short conversation, I realised that he had passed the unwritten test of 'a suitable young man', and we were free to walk round the corner to where the car was parked.

Even I could see that it was a vintage automobile: a bull-nosed Morris Oxford with a canvas roof and very high off the ground. Nigel opened the door and helped me in – another plus mark for a gentleman. Then he pulled out the choke and inserted a penny. "When the engine catches you must pull it out immediately. Otherwise the engine will flood."

As a non-driver, I didn't know what he was talking about, but he went round to the front and began cranking the starting handle. The engine failed to 'catch'. By now we had collected a few small boys who had been playing football in our quiet suburban street.

"Do you have to wind your car up?" one enquired.

"My dad's car starts with a button," chirped another.

"Is it clockwork?" queried the first.

Luckily, on the next swing of the starting handle, the engine fired. I snatched the penny, dropping it on the floor. Nigel leapt into the driver's seat and we were away.

It was impossible to talk above the racket. I couldn't see the penny on the floor and wondered how we would start the car for our journey home if such a vital piece of equipment were missing. The car was probably a death trap but this was before the days of MOTs, so Nigel drove it with impunity. Today such a vehicle would be lovingly restored for car rallies, but back then it was simply his transport.

I realised I hadn't asked where we were going, but recognised the villages as we passed. Then we turned off a minor road on to an even narrower one with grass in the middle. After about a mile, Nigel slowed and took an abrupt left turn through a couple of stone pillars onto an even rougher drive. We bounced from rut to rut for what seemed a long time until an enormous but beautiful Jacobean mansion came into sight.

Nigel drove round the side into a stable yard and stopped the car. I scrabbled about on the floor, found the penny and gave it to him as he helped me out of the vehicle. We entered through a rear door and went down a maze of musty stone passages. I was beginning to wonder where this was leading when we arrived in a cavernous kitchen complete with enormous coal-fired range and masses of sinks with wooden draining boards. Then we followed another passage with a runner along the corridor, rows of bells up by the ceiling and doors on both sides. We arrived at an actual green baize door and entered the vast hall.

"This way," Nigel called from a double door as I was gazing round the impressive room and staircase. He opened the door to another large room, but this time it was light because of the floor-to-ceiling windows down one side and opposite the enormous fireplace.

The next thing to catch my eye was a very long dining table. Instead of being where you would expect it, down the centre of the room, it was placed to stretch from the fireplace to the centre of the three French windows. Halfway down it between at least eight chairs were some library steps.

Seated at the table by the window and reading a newspaper was Nigel's father. As he put the paper down, I recognised the Lord Lieutenant. I had seen him at numerous official functions but knew he would not know me. He rose courteously to greet me; the dogs round his feet gave a more effusive welcome. We made some small talk. Then he muttered something about seeing to something and went out of the room, calling to the dogs who bustled off behind him.

"Nigel, you didn't say," was all I could think of.

"I didn't want to put you off too soon," he answered.

Of course his surname would be different from his father's because he was a peer of the realm, and I had made no connection, especially as Nigel didn't use his 'Honourable' title.

I looked again at the long table. It was obvious that this was the room where Nigel and his father lived. Now that it was summer, they had established themselves at the window end of the table where there were piles of newspapers and scattered books. The next couple of chairs down was obviously the place where they ate breakfast; the marmalade pots remained in the centre of the table. The adjacent area was 'office' as I could see piles of papers and envelopes and a large blotter with an inkstand and pens. Next there was a dusty area with footprints on the table and by the library steps. Further up the table and nearer the fireplace was the part presumably used in the winter, with sherry decanters and glasses, more books and more clutter.

"Would you like to see the rest of the house?" he asked. I nodded and was amazed that instead of edging round the end of the table, Nigel walked to the middle and strode up the steps, over the table and down a matching set on the other side. He waited as I did the same, hoping my stiletto heels would not mark the unpolished wood, and he courteously helped me down the steps on the far side and out into another reception room.

The house was just as large as I expected. Obviously most of the rooms weren't used; dust covers that had once been white were over most of the furniture. The pictures of ancestors lined every wall and the stairs and watched me with curious eyes. Nigel was an amusing guide as he told me family anecdotes and made the portraits come to life, describing who each person was and what they had done as if they were still alive instead of most dead for hundreds of years.

We ended up at the kitchen. He pulled a kettle over the enormous range and brewed us a cup of tea in an oversized, slightly stained china pot. But it was very embarrassing when, having gulped the last of his cup, he got down on one knee and proposed marriage.

The old kitchen was an incongruous and most unromantic setting. Nigel was so earnest, his proposal so formal and so utterly inappropriate and unexpected. It took me completely by surprise.

My first instinct was to laugh but I didn't want to hurt his feelings, so I took a deep breath and talked my way out of the situation. I tried to explain that I really hardly knew him, I never thought he might want me to be his wife and other stupid remarks, all to put off the moment when I would have to refuse.

"I'll use the handle to my name again, and it will be yours too," he said.

Handle? Oh – title! No thank you.

"We were so natural as girlfriend and boyfriend in *The Hollow*," he pleaded. "I want it to be for life too."

Although he was very sweet, he clearly didn't live in the same world that I inhabited. His house, despite its air of faded grandeur, would be so cold and uncomfortable to live in – much like the rest of his life, I guessed. But I did say 'no', rather definitely. The drive home was in uncomfortable silence and I realised that we were not going to be friends any more either.

NIGEL'S MANSION was eventually sold to developers who turned it into a convalescent home. He and his father continued to live in the grounds, in a small house. As time went by, he inherited the title and took his seat in the House of Lords. He never married.

Once in a while, over the years, I caught myself daydreaming about what life might have been like had I instead said 'yes' – and shuddered at the thought. The worst realisation was that all the newspapers and magazines I had worked for, all the freelance commissions I had completed, the editorships, all the work that I love doing which has kept me occupied all my life – to say nothing of a long, eventful and happy marriage, two daughters and six grandchildren – wouldn't have happened. What a bore.

In trying to let him down gently, I had told Nigel that I really liked my job and to marry him, I would have to give it up, as the *Herald* didn't employ married women. He looked at me incredulously. "My wife could never have paid employment outside the home," was his stiff reply.

I suspect, had I moved into that grand house, that sooner rather than later I would have been making the news, not reporting it – for all the wrong reasons – under a tabloid headline like 'HE DROVE ME TO IT' CLAIMS HUSBAND KILLER.

Young women of my generation were intent on breaking the mould that poor Nigel's generation of the upper class were trying in vain to force us into. I think we did a pretty good job of it.